The End of
THE LINE

The End of THE LINE

The Last Ten Years at Swindon Works

Ron Bateman

The History Press

Front Cover Illustrations: Redundant railway workers march across Waterloo Bridge, August 1983 (Tony Rima); the dismantling and scrapping of the A-Shop, 1987 (Brian Robert Marshall).

Back Cover Illustration: Rail workers listen to John Prescott at Farrindon Road Park, 4 August 1984 (Andy Binks, The Swindon Society).

First published 2020

The History Press
97 St George's Place, Cheltenham,
Gloucestershire, GL50 3QB
www.thehistorypress.co.uk

British Library Cataloguing in Publication Data.
A catalogue record for this book is available from the British Library.

ISBN 978 0 7509 9312 8

Typesetting and origination by The History Press
Printed and bound in Great Britain by TJ International Ltd.

MIX
Paper from responsible sources
FSC® C013056
FSC www.fsc.org

CONTENTS

This publication of this book commemorates the sixtieth anniversary of the completion of 92220 *Evening Star* in March 1960. Built in Swindon Works, she was the final steam locomotive for British Railways.

Evening Star and the men who built her. Also see the images in the colour section. (Andy Binks, The Swindon Society)

FOREWORD

BR Standard Class 9F 92220 is more than just a steam locomotive. Swindon Works was more than just a railway factory. Both are much bigger than the sum of their parts. Both have a rich heritage and presence that still lives on today. The sixtieth anniversary of the *Evening Star* is an appropriate time to revisit that heritage and explore the nuts and bolts of the calibre of the men who built her, as well as their fight to keep Swindon 'railway'.

No. 92220 *Evening Star* has many credentials that make it special: it was named by a competition, it was the last steam locomotive built by BR and at Swindon Works, and it was built for preservation. It is a living reminder of a bygone age.

The rich railway heritage that was Swindon is still visible today, if you know where to look for it. Hidden under the layers of 'other' uses, incomers, as Swindonians called those who had not been born and bred in Swindon, would be hard pressed to know its original purpose. In the decades between Swindon Works' closure on 'Black Wednesday', 26 March 1986 to now, Swindon has changed from a town filled with railwaymen and women and their families, almost totally reliant on the railways, whether Great Western Railway or British Rail, 'to a thriving economic centre of commerce and multinational expansion' and the railway factory with its myriad of old workshops now serves its community in different ways, so that only those 'who were there' know the reality of what it really was and what made it so great that its reputation was worldwide and is still talked of today.

Whilst most of the old buildings stand proud and strong, many of those 'insider' witnesses have passed on. Indeed, a great many of those older railwaymen who I interviewed to record their stories and experiences are, sadly, no longer here. Now they need the younger generation that followed them from the era of steam to the time of diesel and electrical trains to record those stories and those times. Happily, those of the BR era are still here with memories and recollections that are as fresh and vital as on the first day they stepped inside the works.

In this fascinating exploration of the works' demise from the late 1970s, Ron Bateman explores his own experiences and recollections alongside those of his railway workmates and 'railway family'. Starting with his time in the Works Training School (WTS), then as 'the boy' apprentice painter before working as a skilled coach painter mainly in the huge A Shop working on the electrical multiple units for the Kent Coast routes, until eventually joining the last few men on 'the funeral cortege' of the final day in 1986, he tells of the ups but mostly downs as the works and its men fought for their existence.

Those interested in either railway, social, economic, or trade union history will find this an intriguing step back 'inside' those famous Swindon Works walls, and although it was 'the End of the Line' it is the beginning of a great read.

Dr Rosa Matheson

INTRODUCTION

The closure of Swindon's former Great Western Railway Works was arguably the most significant milestone in the history of the town. The Great Western Railway (GWR) has long been regarded by railway enthusiasts as 'the stuff of legends', and during its heyday the Swindon Works built some of the most powerful steam locomotives in the world. At its peak in the mid-1920s it was staffed by more than 14,000 employees, and in 1919, following a much-needed programme of expansion, the mighty A Shop became Europe's largest building under one roof. Former Works Manager Harry Roberts summed up Swindon's role in the GWR beautifully when he proclaimed that Swindon locomotives had been designed and built to become 'trend-setters and world-leaders – hence the adaptation of GWR into God's Wonderful Railway'.[1]

Had it not been for its former dependence on the GWR company, the town of Swindon would probably not have evolved into the large-scale urban development of around 250,000 inhabitants that exists today. From the day the works opened in 1843, a marked demographic increase kept pace with the gradual expansion of the works. Over the next twenty years the population increased from 2,500 to more than 7,000, and by 1911 to around 51,000, with nearly a quarter of this figure employed inside the town's railway workshops.[2] Swindon Works also played an active role in respect of the education, welfare and recreational opportunities of its employees. In comparison with the surrounding area, because of this almost exclusive dependence on railway employment, Swindon came to be regarded as being differentiated – economically, socially and culturally.

A CULTURE OF BELONGING

Across almost a century and a half of continuous operation, no fewer than six generations of workers drawn from Swindon and the surrounding area went inside to earn their living. A large number of those men could boast a generation-upon-generation connection to the works through their fathers, their grandfathers and even their great-grandfathers. They spoke with unbridled passion about the glory days of steam, and typically viewed the Swindon Works as the centre of their universe; especially those who remembered the dominant role that the works used to play at the very heart of the town's active life. Even throughout those final ten years that are the subject of this book, those of us who went inside at that eleventh hour still initially developed a sense of pride that we were carrying on the tradition of half a dozen previous generations of 'Swindonians' who had proudly served their time in the railway works. It is also apparent from the many comments that I have either read or listened to in the course of this exercise that numerous former employees look back on their service in the workshops with great fondness – describing it as 'the best place I ever worked' in so many cases. The camaraderie inside the works was the chief aspect that the men particularly liked to reflect upon. It is something that still carries on more than three decades after the works closed, particularly at regular coffee mornings in the Railway Village Community Centre. 'The spirit and camaraderie inside the works was phenomenal! Everyone still has it. Everyone still looks out for each other.'[3]

When I began my apprenticeship in the autumn of 1977, I had at first been overwhelmed by the history and traditions of the Swindon Works, as well as being touched by the sentimentality of the men who had served in the works back in the days of the Great Western Railway. I quickly came to realise that the aura of romance that embellished the days of the GWR had never fully faded. The men who had previously worked for the company, and then later for British Rail (BR) were very proud men, many of whom were happy to admit that they 'lived' to serve in the works. I was also particularly impressed by the dedication and professionalism of many of the staff employed at the Works Training School – particularly those instructors who came across from the works to teach us health and safety and first-aid procedures. They lived and breathed Swindon Works, and they gradually indoctrinated us into a culture that they obviously adored. It was as clear to me then as it is now that they had all internalised a proud sense of 'belonging' that seemed to permeate every aspect of their lives. This was true across many generations of 'Swindonians' whose service in the railway works was proudly woven into their family histories, just as the importance of the works is now deeply embedded in the history of the town.

Every generation of school-leavers who went inside quickly became absorbed into this exclusive micro-culture, a shared perspective that included a medium of slang unique to Swindon Works that stretched back across many generations. When asked to define that culture well over three decades later, I find it difficult to provide an explanation that can be condensed into a single sentence. It was a culture that went beyond that shared vocabulary; it was more like being part of a brotherhood or an extended family. It had as much to do with shared ideas and values, a sense of community and comradeship, and of doing an honest day's work and having pride in the work that was done. It also had something to do with shared involvement in sporting and social functions or other after-hours activities, and of serving the establishment in ways that were in addition to the job itself. At its most base level, the rail works culture went beyond being an instinctive adherence to a certain way of life. Being a 'true railwayman' incorporated a deep sense of belonging to the works, just as an animal belongs to its habitat. Having since taken this opportunity to work through the chronology of events leading up to the decline and closure of the works, it seems amazing to me just how resilient that 'rail works culture' turned out to be. Despite nationalisation, despite the end of the steam era and despite the headcount reductions of the 1960s that saw the size of the workforce shrink alarmingly, the culture of the rail works continued to survive – undiluted by the effects of deliberate disinvestment.

I vividly remember my first real insight into that 'culture of belonging' on the day I was taken on my first guided tour of Swindon Works in the early spring of 1978. Aside from my amazement at discovering what lay beyond those tall, red brick walls, the other thing that struck me was that many of the workshops incorporated communal areas for the various 'gangs' that often had a home-from-home appearance. I remember on those first wanderings through the great archipelago of workshops that one could not help but notice the occasional fish tank, the odd cat hanging around here and there, and the well-stocked larder hidden behind a 'Rail Blue' cupboard door. I also noticed the chinaware and cutlery, the electric heaters, the shaving facilities, the mirrors, the kettles, the glazed, earthenware teapots, the neat tables, the magazine racks, the house plants, the ornamental clocks and barometers and the radios. These kinds of things were a long way from the kind of factory life that I had expected or imagined. Nor did I ever expect to see sparrows flying freely around the workshops, and piles of crumbs laid out on factory-issue blue paper for the purpose of feeding the uninvited guests. More importantly, I was never under any illusion that such home comforts distracted the men from the most important thing – that being the job in hand. These men were happy to spend their entire working life inside, and these added comforts and amusements were just another extension of the deep sense of belonging that existed within Swindon Works.

BLACK FRIDAYS AND THE END OF THE GWR

Those of us who went inside during that final decade of the works still possess very vivid memories of watching close to a century and a half of railway engineering history dying before our eyes. Even though we were at 'the sharp end' of it, the critical events that brought about the demise and death of the works can be viewed as having occurred over a long period of time in three distinct phases. It is worth looking back briefly, if only to appreciate just how we got to where we were at the beginning of that final ten-year period.

After eighty-odd years of almost unbroken success, the Great Western Railway Company had first run into severe difficulties during the interwar period, mainly due to the collapse of the Welsh coal trade in the years following the General Strike of 1926. Additionally, the ever-expanding road transport network would bring about an end to an era of guaranteed dominance and prosperity for the company. The GWR would be compelled to economise wherever possible – even to the extent that a storeman would not issue a new broom until he was satisfied that the bristles on the old one were sufficiently worn![4] Eventually there were major job losses at the works in the 1930s when profits began to fall alarmingly. In his book about Swindon Works in the 1930s, Hugh Freebury writes of the dreaded 'Black Fridays' when foremen emerged from their offices with lists of workers to be released.[5] Anxiety-fuelled rumours that the workload had dropped off would begin to circulate weeks in advance, and soon everyone would be convinced that a large number of workers would have to be let go. The consequences of such a thing would have been far more devastating in the 1930s as Swindon was much more of a one-industry town and being laid off would all but condemn a man to the breadline. There just wasn't the same level of governmental support back then, and neither would the men have received any assistance from the company, except a promise that, 'You can come back when things are looking up again.' Men whose fathers had been inside had grown up with the recurring threat of redundancy hanging over the household, and soon they themselves would be suffering a similar fate. Freebury writes of the 'partiality and favouritism' employed by the foremen in the early days, a system that allowed them to retain or get rid of whoever they wanted. The emerging might of the unions had recently put paid to such practices, and their insistence of 'last in, first out' had at the very least put some minds at rest. To the men who worked inside throughout the final years of the works, this all sounds very familiar, except in our case at least we would have a fighting chance of getting another job locally, or would at least be offered opportunities for retraining, along with a fixed allowance and state aid if we passed the means test. For those men in the 1930s, the best they could hope for was a job in another town or city involving a long commute, or else scraping by on a means-tested benefit that barely allowed for basic subsistence.

The GWR company struggled on thereafter and was given a much-needed boost when figures spiked again immediately after the war when petrol shortages and rationing worked in its favour.[6] This improvement in its fortunes allowed the GWR to partially recover from the ravages of war, before finally succumbing to nationalisation in 1948; thereafter it became the Western Region of British Rail. The iconic designs and livery of the GWR continued to be used for a number of years afterwards, despite the company having being officially wound up in December 1949.

EVENING STAR: THE HARBINGER OF DOOM?

A second feature that can be said to have exacerbated the decline of Swindon Works was a brutal programme of cuts to the railway network in the 1960s. It was a process that not only sought to accelerate the phasing out of the steam locomotive but would also result in the end of locomotive manufacturing in Swindon – the very thing on which the proud reputation of the works had been built. This procedure had already begun to occur in the decade following nationalisation when the Modernisation Plan of 1955 called for the complete phasing out of steam traction. Even though British Rail overly pessimistically forecasted that this could not be fully achieved before 1972, it was still a hammer blow for the works. The psychological effect that the end of steam locomotive manufacture created – the realisation that those magnificent engines that gave us our 'glow of pride' were now gone forever – never really receded. It is for this reason that this memoir has been released to coincide with the sixtieth anniversary of the final steam locomotive to be built at Swindon Works – or anywhere by British Rail – the 9F freight locomotive No. 92220 *Evening Star.*

I remember as a boy being fascinated by the *Evening Star* – I had never seen a locomotive with five pairs of coupled driving wheels beneath such a huge boiler. I also remember as an apprentice utilising one of my free railway passes to travel up to York one day just to stand and admire it in the National Railway Museum. Despite the fact that Swindon's railmen had staged a one-day strike in 1958 after British Rail had said an order for ten 9Fs could not be built in the works, the *Evening Star* was not held in the same reverence by many of the former GWR men that I came into contact with. They would speak with passion and pride about the magnificence of the GWR Castles and Kings, but the *Evening Star* – despite its name – did not shine so brightly. I remember one embittered craftsman from the age of steam insisting that this giant locomotive was a 'white elephant' and scoffed that its cost had far outweighed its usefulness. All the indications at the time seemed to suggest that *Evening Star* was being built solely for the purpose of future preservation. Its production had been delayed by three years due to the accelerated introduction of the ill-fated Warship Class 42 diesel-hydraulic locomotives – a development that merely added to the cynicism. Diesel manufacture had long been in progress, and yet here they were, building another steam locomotive, while men in the same works were employed outside in the yard in breaking them up for scrap!

It also seemed to be a strange thing to be doing, bearing in mind the financial position of British Rail at that time, as this did not make impressive reading. The passenger side posted a loss of £87.7 million in 1960, while the freight side lost £46 million. When adjusted to take into account a slight profit in the parcels division, BR posted total losses of £128.3 million

– hardly the time to be spending a huge sum on building a soon-to-be obsolete locomotive![7] Figures from 1960 onwards also reflected a constrained demand for rail transport, while at the same time a massively expanding motorway network over the next decade and a half ultimately gave rise to a new age of road transport.

It is now an accepted fact that *Evening Star* had indeed been built by British Rail with a view to preservation status, and was never intended to serve out its useful life. Workers were given food for thinking as such when a competition was organised to find a name for the locomotive – the only 9F that was officially named. Three entrants had all chosen the name that BR thought appropriate, owing to the fact that one of the first locomotives to operate on the GWR had been named *Morning Star*. To enhance its appearance for preservation *Evening Star* was also given a specially commissioned livery and copper-capped chimney – all the other 250 9F locomotives were painted black.

A special naming ceremony for *Evening Star* was to be held in the AE Shop at Swindon Works on 18 March 1960. The foreword in the programme for the ceremony stated that:

> The Building at the Swindon Works of British Rail last steam locomotive marks the end of an era begun by Watt, Trevithick and Stephenson, and the onrush of modernisation by which diesel and electric traction become the impelling force on the country's railways. This ceremony is held fittingly to praise steam as a medium by which untold millions of miles have been run in the service of humanity, and through which British Rail developed a network of railways second to none in the world.

The historical and emotional significance of the final steam locomotive was alluded to by R.F. Hanks of the British Transport Commission, who chose his words carefully for the occasion:

> I trust I shall not be considered parochial when I say that it is a proud day for Great Western men everywhere who will find much satisfaction, since there had to be a 'last one' that it should fall to the lot of Swindon to see the job through.
>
> We must not be gloomy today, but thankful that steam has served the railways so long and so faithfully.

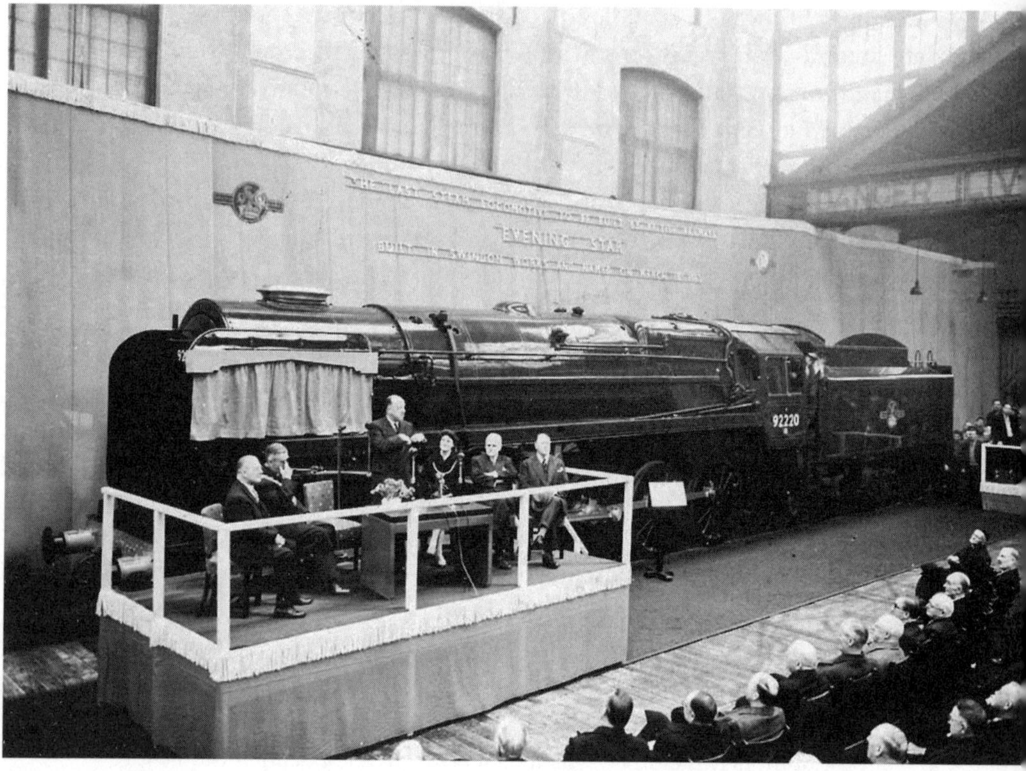

R.F. Hanks of the British Transport Commission chose his words carefully at the naming ceremony for 92220 *Evening Star*. (*Swindon Advertiser*)

The former General Manager of the Western Region, K.W.C Grand, then presented the three winners of the naming competition with their share of the ten-Guinea prize.[8] Meanwhile, David Gilles was an engineering apprentice in A Shop back in 1960, and witnessed the ceremony from the farthest track of the 100-ton crane:

> I took a photo just after the curtains had been opened by KWC Grand to officially reveal the name of 92220, which of course, was no surprise to us. I believe the locomotive was in light steam and made not a sound during the entire ceremony. Afterwards I recall a 204hp diesel shunter dragging it out of the AE Shop because its boiler pressure had dropped too low.[9]

One veteran of the works who declined to be named remembered making the ash pans for the *Evening Star*, and also remembered the naming ceremony:

> It was all very sad really. The works made a big effort to turn it into a celebration, rather than the sad occasion that it was. They brought in some of the famous locos from Swindon's glorious past – some great names that had gone before. The *North Star* was there, another locomotive we built for the Caledonian Railways and also the *City of Truro* – they were all displayed in the workshop for the occasion.

One railwayman with forty-six years inside looked on with sadness and made his feelings known to the *Evening Advertiser*, which gave the ceremony front-page exposure:

> The new day had to come, but so much is lost too. There was romance in the sight and smell of steam. The scent of the old steam engine had memories for all of us, but they will soon be something long gone.

Evening Advertiser, 18 March 1960

Fred Simpson had started out at Swindon Works as an office boy in 1935, before getting a job on the footplate two years later. He spent fifteen years as a fireman and twenty-two years a driver, and tested out *Evening Star* while it was still painted black, before getting a final coat of the famous Brunswick Green. It was around this time that Fred had to switch over to testing diesel locomotives:

> The switch over to diesel locomotives was not popular. We accepted the change – we thought it was great and clean and warm. But driving was strange being on your own. It eventually became a bore – you no longer had the adrenaline when going at 70 or 80mph.

Swindon Advertiser, 1 April 2006

A few days after the naming ceremony, on 21 March, a peal referred to as *Evening Star Delight Minor* was rung at St Marks Church for more than two and a half hours to mark the completion of the final steam locomotive.[10]

Stephenson's *Rocket* and *Evening Star,* special naming ceremony programme, 18 March 1960.

If the completion of the *Evening Star* was deemed to be an event worthy of celebration, there would be very little else to celebrate at Swindon Works for the next seventeen years. Following the Main Workshops for the Future Plan of 1962 that called for closure of fifteen of the thirty-one railway workshops in the country, the old carriage and wagon works in Swindon was earmarked for closure by 1967. This initiative was given further impetus by Beeching's plans for reduction and restructuring Britain's railways outlined in two reports in 1963 and 1965. The Beeching Axe, as it became known, would decimate Britain's railway network through the elimination of many uneconomical services in an effort to make it profitable. Beeching's determined assault raised the tempo of major cutbacks, which had a significant impact on the headcount at Swindon Works. The workforce effectively halved, coming down from more than 8,000 in 1963 to 4,203 in 1965 and then to 3,886 by 1969.[11] Nationally, the number of workshops was cut by twelve between 1962 and 1966, coupled with significant reductions in the remaining nationwide workforce. From 1 January 1963, control of all of the regions' main workshops would thereafter be transferred to one central authority called the British Railways Workshop Division, a move that was widely considered to have been a bad thing for Swindon Works. Throughout the regions as stations were closed and railway lines were torn from their sleepers in accordance with the plan, Beeching also asserted that the British Transport Commission had been overly pessimistic in its forecast that all steam locomotives could not be fully phased out until 1972, and proposed a significant acceleration of the process. All steam locos would be withdrawn from both the East and Western Regions by 1965; and from all other regions by 1967. As things turned out there would be no more steam after August 1968.[12]

Suspicion about *Evening Star*'s limited lifespan was realised when the locomotive was officially withdrawn from service just five years after the naming ceremony. The locomotive was thereafter kept in operational service until well into the 1980s, having been claimed for the national collection in 1975.[13] With regular maintenance, steam engines typically lasted for thirty years, although the Class Fs such as *Evening Star* had been designed to last for twenty. In the same year that the locomotive was withdrawn prematurely, the remaining 5,000 or so workers in Swindon were dealt yet another hammer blow when the announcement came that Swindon Works would no longer build railway locomotives. The decision by the Western Region management to take the path of experimenting with diesel-hydraulic transmission had turned out to be a grave error when Beeching discarded the system in favour of diesel-electric locomotion. It was felt that a degree of favouritism had come into play here, for the costs of converting from steam to this type of diesel, whereby the wheels were powered by engine rotation, had not weighed too heavily on the works' budget, although large bonuses recently negotiated in favour of Swindon workers had not helped their cause.[14] British Rail began the withdrawal of the Class 14 diesel-hydraulic locomotives in 1968, and by 1970 none remained. The Warship Class 42 locomotives were all withdrawn between 1968 and 1972.

The now redundant former locomotive works would be reconditioned and modified to allow for carriage and wagon repair. The loss of locomotive manufacture came as a terrible blow to the workforce as there were many employees at the time who believed that 'dieselisation' would be

Obsolete diesel-hydraulic locomotives scattered around the yard at Swindon Works in 1975 prior to being broken up for scrap. (Ron Bateman Snr)

Commemorative plaque attached to the boiler casing of *Evening Star*. (Ron Bateman)

the beginning of a bright new future for the works. Going forward, they could only seek reassurance from the fact that Swindon still had its carriage and wagon works. A number of veterans I spoke to from this era still felt bitter about this, and felt this was a much bigger blow than the phasing out of steam traction. One former foreman in the AE Shop thought the Warships were superb locomotives, 'It was the Maybach engines that were the problem.' As simple as this may sound, neither the Warships, nor the Western Class locomotives, were all fitted with Maybach engines. There are differing perspectives on which manufacturers' engines were to blame.[15]

Evening Star returned to its place of birth in April of 1990 as a part of the 'National Railway Museum on Tour' exhibition staged in the old 19 Shop in Swindon Works. It returned again in September 2008, and remained on display for two years at the Swindon Steam Museum of the GWR to celebrate the fiftieth anniversary of its completion. By this time, the dark significance of the 999th BR Standard locomotive had long been forgiven by the railway enthusiasts, many of whom turned up in their thousands to marvel at the beauty and size of such an impressive feat of railway engineering.

FROM HOPE TO DESPAIR – THE FINAL DECADE

The third and final phase in the demise brings us to *The End of the Line: The Last Ten Years of Swindon Works*. Armed with so many memories and so much information, I have written this account as an attempt to both chronicle and to share my experience of that final ten years inside. The early chapters reflect a period that began on a note of real optimism when the works unexpectedly won a contract to build complete locomotives for the first time in twelve years. In the intervening years, which had seen the withdrawal of the diesel-hydraulic fleet in the early 1970s, the shop floor headcount had fallen perilously low to just 1,800 manual workers, with only around 2,200 on the payroll in total. By that time, the old British Transport Commission and been disbanded, to be replaced by the British Railways Board. Then, on 1 January 1970, British Rail Engineering Ltd (BREL) was formed as a subsidiary company of British Rail, and it was then that a new Work's Manager, Yorkshireman Harry Roberts arrived on the scene, cast in the role of 'the axeman' by his impatient employers.

Harry Roberts presents the apprentice of the year shield in 1973. Roberts had arrived at Swindon in 1972 with a remit to close the works. (Roy Hazell Collection)

> My own arrival at the works in July 1972 was not exactly heralded with a fanfare of trumpets, as it was an open secret that my remit was to close the works down completely – the quicker the better as far as the BR board were concerned!
>
> Harry Roberts, 1985

Roberts quickly absorbed what he described as, 'The true potential obscured under the disorientated, disordered atmosphere that pervaded the whole works,' and, against the demands of his employer, endeavoured to keep the Swindon Works operational for as long as possible. By 1977, under his guidance, the works started winning new orders for outside work that brought a fresh wave of optimism as the headcount began to increase once more. Roberts achieved this by actively promoting the efficiency of the works, and was thereafter rewarded with a string of orders that would stave off the dreaded axe for the foreseeable future. During that ensuing period of calm when the ship held steady for a number of years we were able to laugh and joke together, and to make plans – even going as far as to buy houses, marry our girlfriends and start families! Had Roberts seen things differently at that time, my life would have taken a completely different direction, and I would not have had a final ten years inside Swindon Works to write about.

Sadly, the upsurge in confidence in the late 1970s was not to last, and for all his genuine effort on our behalf, Harry Roberts had only been able to buy us some time. By the early 1980s, anyone but the politically naïve would have become increasingly aware that the favoured 'New Right' ideology of the Thatcher government would finally spell the end for the railway workshops. Thatcherism encompassed a commitment to a new economic liberalism, resulting in policies that included privatisation of nationalised industries. The Serpell Review of 1982–83 – a commission of enquiry set up to examine ways of improving railway finances – agreed that privatisation would be an option worthy of consideration as far as BREL was concerned. Although the review had been widely rejected by the government, it was soon being accused of implementing the recommendations by stealth. Government policy thereafter would incorporate an insistence that replacement and refurbishment of BR's ageing rolling stock be procured wherever possible by means of competitive tendering, a clear indication that the main rationale was to prepare railway engineering for privatisation.[16] For Swindon Works, primarily a repair and refurbishment facility, this would indeed mean that the end of the line was more than a distinct possibility.

When I had completed my apprenticeship (or 'came out of my time' as it was known), I was immediately re-employed as a tradesman painter, and within a year the renewed optimism that had permeated the atmosphere when I first began my apprenticeship in the late 1970s had long since faded. The later chapters of this book describe what evolved into a long downward spiral for the works, a period largely characterised by consecutive headcount reductions. The forward planning of BREL had reflected a desire for new build and modernisation over repair and refurbish, a strategy that undoubtedly paid heed to the government's privatisation ambition. For the worker, it was about the constant vacillation between hope to despair, and about trying to get on with one's life, albeit on the edge of a deep ravine that was constantly being referred to as 'outside in the real world'. This was an existence I had endured for much of the first ten years of my working life, for the first six years of my then married life and for my first three years as a father.

From April 1982 onwards the road to that infamous Black Wednesday became a long, demoralising journey, largely endured in an atmosphere of rancour and cynicism as the ongoing fight to save Swindon Works became ever more bitter. There were no more significant orders in the pipeline, men were succumbing to early retirement and voluntary redundancy on an almost daily basis and the workshops were looking increasingly bare.

Just as the overall decline of Swindon works can be separated out into three distinct phases, so the process of running down and eventually closing the works also encompassed three key stages of headcount reduction. Some of the figures quoted in the local press and by employees' representatives are at first confusing, as they seldom kept in step with the numbers and pace of the ongoing headcount reductions originally planned. As virtually all the surplus employees pertaining to the first two headcount reductions took either early retirement or volunteered for redundancy, it is difficult to know exactly how many employees had effectively been let go prior to the next phase of job losses being announced. Additionally, some of the figures quoted often related only to shop floor men, and did not take into account the office staff and other employees indirectly connected to the works. The only certainty was that my turn would soon come, and along with many hundreds of my rail works colleagues I had to accept that my not too distant fate would be to find myself jobless at a time of mass unemployment both locally and nationally.

When the decision to close the works finally came, it still felt like a crushing blow, even though it had long been expected. It was not just the personal ramifications of the decision that hit home either, it was also the realisation that 143 years of railway engineering in the town was going to end in a matter of months. I still remember the bitterness felt by my colleagues when all was lost, and the ghostly atmosphere inside the deserted workshops on the night shift during those final weeks. People who had been employed at the works, in some cases for their entire working life,

Formerly a hive of activity, the now deserted AM shop prior to demolition. (Jason McCormick/Neil Lover, Swindon's Other Railway)

were simply discarded, owing to what British Rail described as 'over-riding business problems'.[17] Black Wednesday was a day that will live in infamy for those who were there, when the silence was so deafening that one could barely gather ones thoughts. Barely a quarter of a century after *Evening Star* had entered service, Swindon's railway works was effectively consigned to the history books.

A PERSONAL MEMOIR OF LIFE ON THE INSIDE

Most of my own personal memories in this account were rough drafted around twenty-eight years ago, just a few years after the works had officially closed down. The idea to put into print everything that I could remember from my time inside had originally come to me when I first read Hugh Freebury's excellent *Great Western Apprentice: Swindon in the Thirties*, a classic, active participant account of what day-to-day life in the works was really like.[18] Freebury writes of his experiences with such emotional openness that one internalises his thoughts and his feelings, his hopes and his regrets and his highs and his lows. His motivation for writing the book had been to tell the other side of the story, that being from the shop-floor perspective. Large-scale reductions in headcount had occurred in the Swindon Works during the 1930s, and he felt as though the worry and the hardship endured by large numbers of embittered men had been understated in an account that had recently been published by a member of the management team.[19] I took inspiration from his references to many of the familiar phrases and rituals with which I was familiar, and began setting down my own memories of my time as a British Rail apprentice and tradesman in what were similarly difficult times.

Well over a quarter of a century has now passed since I wrote those memoirs, a period that included two divorces and various house moves; little wonder I had long since thought the manuscript to be lost. It was only during my preparations to relocate overseas in early 2016 that I rediscovered much of the original typescript that I had drafted all those years ago. Upon re-reading, it immediately became apparent to me that, even in its slightly juvenile form, it really did capture something of the atmosphere inside the Swindon Works throughout those final ten years. The memoir also contained a detailed account of my time at the Works Training School, an exercise that at that time had never been published before. I had no serious ambition to be a writer back in 1991, so I presumably wrote everything down under the assumption that in years to come my memories of my apprenticeship and of working inside would fade, destined to become distorted by the fallibility of long-term memory. At the time I simply wanted to preserve my own memories of the works by telling my own story to myself – exactly how I remembered it. I have since edited that original document as an attempt to describe, evaluate and chronicle the experiences and observations of which I originally wrote. I have also readily taken on board the experiences of others, sometimes as a means of providing a measure of verification to my own recollections.

Having now described that 'journey', the end result represents a unique angle on the experience of being inside the Swindon Works throughout that final decade of its existence. It is evident that in my quest to provide the most truthful interpretation of that original script there was very little danger of too much sentimentality breeding the opposite of fact in the final account. These had been long, stressful years of uncertainty; a period that deeply affected everybody, young and old, and in different ways, especially as the final closure approached. Whatever impression I may create at the conclusion of this memoir, it does not alter the fact that I have always been extremely proud of Swindon's railway heritage. With that in mind, it has never been my intention to rob either the men of the Great Western Railway of their hard-earned glory or those latterly employed by British Rail Engineering Ltd of their remarkable achievements in the face of adversity.

A NOTE ON THE TEXT

The original manuscript I typed back in the early 1990s contained the names of many men who I had long-since forgotten, but to whom I could instantly put a face. A lot of men that I mentioned have sadly long-since passed away and I have no wish to tarnish their memory in any way. Also, there are other men who have since moved on in their lives and would probably not wish to be identified. For these reasons I have applied false names to persons referred to in the course of this book, except for those men who I felt were worthy of high praise, and others who played a key managerial role in the history of the Swindon Works.

Regarding the quotes, all contributors were very happy for me to publish their recollections, although some expressed a preference to remain anonymous.

> It was not a job,
> it was a way of life.
>
> Harry Roberts (1985)

1

1977 – A NEW BEGINNING

One Saturday morning in late August 1977 a large buff envelope dropped through our letterbox addressed to Mr Ronald N. Bateman Esquire. I rarely received any mail back then, let alone large buff envelopes addressed with such formal salutation. Little wonder it aroused a considerable amount of interest among the family as I tore it open and withdrew the enclosed documents:

> The Engineering Industry Training Board wishes to inform you that we will undertake to provide the necessary funding for a twelve-month training period at British Rail Engineering Ltd in Swindon. You are therefore invited to report to the Swindon Works Training School in Newburn Crescent at 0800 hours on Monday, 5 September 1977.

I remember my parents warmly congratulated me, probably quite relieved that their second-born had at last ascended to the first rung of the employment ladder and wouldn't be going fishing every day for the rest of his life. 'It's on my way to work, so I can drop you off,' said my dad cheerfully – the same dad who a year or two earlier had pleaded with me, 'Don't just end up in a bloody factory son.'

Although the offer was limited to a twelve-month period, the Engineering Industry Training Board (EITB) was funding this scheme under the expectation that the company with whom the trainee had been placed would agree to fund the remaining three years of the apprenticeship. So in the days that followed my receiving that letter of acceptance, I falsely let it be known that I had been accepted for an apprenticeship at British Rail Engineering Ltd, to which the typical response was, 'At one time, a job in the Swindon Railway Works meant a job for life.' I began to feel slightly deflated by the pessimistic outlook implied by this reaction, for it was a clear indication that the works had been going through a very difficult period in its long, impressive history.

I'd always known that Swindon's history was deeply rooted in the establishment of the Great Western Railway, yet I had remained ignorant throughout my life of anything remotely connected with the ongoing fortunes of the works. As a child, I had assimilated a vague awareness that some famous steam locomotives had been built in Swindon, and through my early schooling I had been made aware that Isambard Kingdom Brunel had made a significant local impact as a brilliant engineer. Sunday morning visits to the Great Western Railway Museum in Farringdon Road with my father still endured in memory, not only for the sight of those magnificent steam engines, but mainly for their wonderful smell – even those that had been stationary for many years! Because those few engines on display were painted dark green, I merely assumed that all steam locomotives were this colour without fully appreciating that this was the famous livery of the Great Western Railway Company. The museum had originally been built as a single men's hostel and was situated adjacent to an area I knew as the Railway Village. Because the railway works was originally situated more than a mile and a half from any means of habitation, an entire village of 300 limestone houses was built to house mainly the married railway workers and their families.

In truth, our family were not really proper 'Swindonians', having moved to Swindon from Bromley in Kent just a few days before I was born. At that time, the mid-1960s, many people from the London suburbs were transferring to 'new towns' in conjunction with various local government 'overspill' schemes. Jobs were being advertised with guaranteed housing included. Apart from those occasional visits to the long-since defunct GWR Museum, I had never set foot in any other building incorporated within the vast network of railway workshops, nor ever had any real appreciation of the colossal importance that the railway works once had to the local communities in and around Swindon. I can remember hearing the famous works hooter on many occasions as a boy and merely assumed that the noise was coming from the fire station. Not until 1977, when my total aversion to staying on at school empowered me to push myself forward for this apprenticeship, did I finally take a keener interest in the Swindon Works.

I had been very fortunate to actually get a craft apprenticeship in 1977, particularly at a time when Swindon had been forced to come to terms with a high degree of economic and social change. By the 1970s Swindon's famous old railway works had long since ceased to be the nucleus of the town's economic life and was now fighting for its very existence. Not only was I completely ignorant of the plight of the railway works but also of the fact that the town had, for many years previously, been going through a steady period of transition characterised by a gradual diversification away from engineering employment. A series of high-profile job losses in manufacturing had occurred in the early 1970s, while at the same time more opportunities were opening up in the world of finance, commerce and service industries.[20] Only years later did it become clear to me that the Swindon Works had been dodging the bullet for a number of years, and was not alone in its capacity as a major manufacturing employer under threat. Many of my fellow railway employees, those who had previously swallowed the bitter pill of redundancy some years previous, had found instant re-employment in car manufacturing, or in Swindon's booming electronics industry. At around this time, however, the most significant job losses in Swindon had taken place within those same establishments – the recently nationalised British Leyland car factory at Pressed Steel Fisher, and also at the electronics giant Plessey Hydraulics and at Garrard Engineering. Most of the job gains were in the service industries, concentrated mainly in financial services and distribution.[21]

Ironically, this meant that throughout the 1970s, despite the fall-off in manufacturing employment, Swindon had begun to acquire a reputation as something of a 'boom town'. An ever-increasing number of large, multinational companies had begun to view the town as the ideal site for setting up administrative headquarters and warehouse facilities. Friends of mine who left school at the same time as me were shunning the idea of going into engineering, instead preferring to seek employment in Hambro Life, Nationwide, W.H. Smith and Burmah Oil – companies that had all recently been headquartered in Swindon. It was fortunate for the town that this transition had taken place in earnest, and its acceleration can be traced back to the completion of the M4 motorway extension, which finally opened in 1971. This effectively tied Swindon into the expanding motorway network, reinforcing its growth potential in terms of regional and national distribution and services. Having sensed a major opportunity, council policy had consciously cultivated this hi-tech M4 corridor image to the benefit of the region.[22] The introduction in the mid-1970s of the High Speed Train (HST), better known as the Inter-City 125, on the main London to Bristol line was equally important, both for business travel back into London and for commuting into Swindon. With an average speed of 92mph, the HST route between the South-West and London provided the fastest regular train service in Britain. By March 1977, the gradual rise in service and financial sector employment was reflected in local unemployment levels of well below the national average.[23] Subsequent demographic increases meant that Swindon was now expanding at an alarming rate.

The railway works rarely hit the local headlines during the mid-1970s, and when it finally did, it was for reasons that had nothing to do with its all too obvious vulnerability. During excavations in the non-ferrous foundry area in 1975, workmen unearthed part of a prehistoric skull. Thereafter, while production continued in the foundry, further excavations revealed many more bones. After consultation with various experts, the bones were identified as belonging to a *Pliosaurus Brachyspondylus*, a very rare sea creature that lived 130–150 million years ago. The sea monster aroused huge interest as it was the most complete skeleton of the animal ever discovered in Britain.[24]

Inside the Swindon Works, the hard core of 2,000 workers that remained seemed largely indifferent to the changing face of Swindon, and probably still never envisaged a life outside of the works. In 1977 it was plain to see that many still considered the railway works to be the principal industry in the town. Maybe this was because they had very recently been given good cause for thinking as such. A rare upturn in the fortunes of Swindon Works in early 1977, at what many people believed to be the 'eleventh hour' for the facility, had ignited a feeling of genuine optimism among the men for the continuing future of the works. The front page of the *Evening Advertiser* for 25 January 1977, carried the headline 'Railworks set to go loco again'. This announcement that Swindon Works was being tipped to win an order to build complete locomotives was reported as 'the biggest shot in the arm the

Left: Pliosaurus Brachyspondylus as laid out for its television debut on *Blue Peter* in 1975. (BRB Residuary)

Below: Artist's impression of the Swindon Works' sea monster. (Giovanni Caselli)

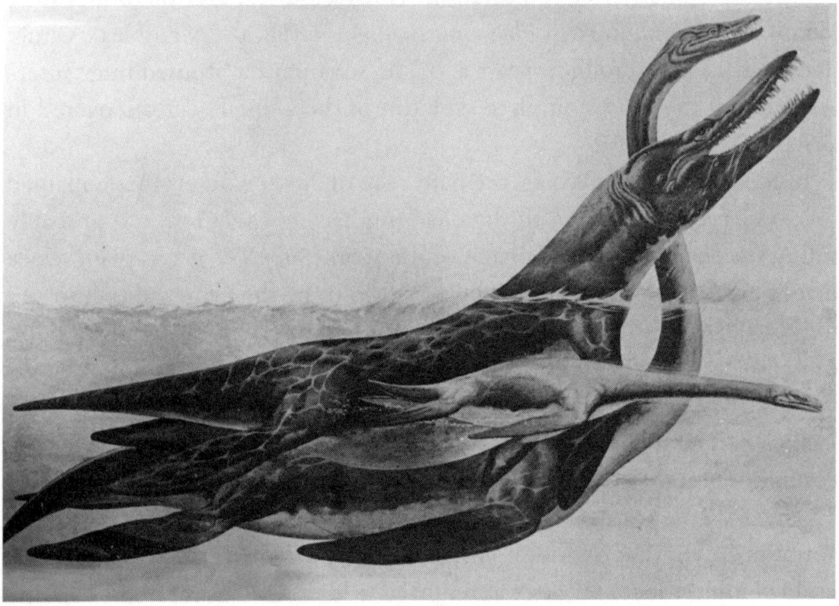

town has had for many years'. This was on the back of a recent order for the partial construction of the thirty Class 56 heavy freight locomotives that was already being undertaken in Swindon. The original order had been won by a Romanian company, however, owing to 'shoddy workmanship' the decision was taken to overhaul the poorly constructed Romanian handiwork and complete the final stages of the work in Swindon.

What really mattered to those inside was that at last the management of the works had finally come out fighting and were now able to pacify the pessimistic element that had been sounding the death knell for the seemingly doomed workshops ever since that aforementioned Beeching Plan of the mid-1960s. Ever since Beeching, a state of dejection, fuelled by a stream of constant negative rumours about the future of the works, had blighted the lives of not only the workers but also the families that employment in the railway works had largely sustained for generations. Now that things were starting to look up, many among the remaining workforce went about their tasks with a renewed feeling of genuine optimism, preferring to believe that this order was the signal for a genuine change of heart within the management structure about the future of Swindon Works. Their optimism was further bolstered by the determination of Works Manager Harry Roberts to offset the general decline in domestic work, which was spelt out very clearly by him in the local press on 25 January 1977: 'If we can build half a locomotive, we can build a complete one. We are looking determinedly at exports and anticipate an explosion of orders from developing countries and intend to see that we get our share.'

If the workers were feeling buoyed by this unexpected piece of news, they would have been near to ecstatic six weeks later when the banner headline article in the local paper read 'Back on the rails'. Swindon Works had been awarded a major share of a £40 million contract to build complete locomotives for the first time since 1965. This hard-won contract to build twenty diesel-hydraulic shunting locomotives for operation on the Kenya Railways network would guarantee employment for a large section of the Swindon workforce for at least a couple more years. Roberts had somehow achieved the impossible by effectively promising the impossible: 'The permitted building time for the shunters had been based on the lead-time to build wagons – not complex diesel-hydraulic locomotives. This meant the lead time was forty percent of a conventional loco-build programme. The other works would not even consider this order.'[25]

Roberts had absolute faith in the ability of the workforce to deliver on the contract. Since his arrival he had fostered an open style of management and cultivated a team spirit and atmosphere that was conducive to attaining all production targets. When the contract between BREL representatives and Hunslet Holdings Limited was signed in Nairobi, a jubilant Roberts declared that, 'Locomotives have come home to Swindon again.'[26] Because it had been so long since complete assembly work had been done in Swindon, fulfilling the contract would involve a degree of retraining as well as bringing an end to certain decades-old demarcation practices. The *Evening Advertiser* commented that the contract would give 'a glow of pride' back to the railway employees in the Swindon Works.[27] The Kenya agreement had multiplied five-fold the value of any outside contract work that the works had won in any previous year. The first of these locomotives was completed on time in January 1979 – the first locomotive to be built in Swindon for fourteen years. It was also the only loco of the consignment to be shipped in the authentic Kenya Railways livery; the remainder were required to be coated only with undercoat primer. The traversing table rails would require modification to a 1m width to accommodate the broader wheel gauge of the new locomotives.[28]

A short while later, the works management were given a further pat on the back for their initiative, courtesy of the town's MP, David Stoddart, when it was announced that an order had been won for seven high-speed oil-rig service boats destined for Nigeria to be manufactured at the works. An impressive reputation for pristine craftsmanship and versatility had won through again for the Swindon workforce. As further orders continued to be won, Roberts would be hailed as the saviour of Swindon Works, as it was mainly through his efforts that it remained in operation right up until 1986. The awarding of a massive contract to overhaul the entire Southern Region commuter fleet in 1979 would guarantee further work for years to come, leading to the recruitment of a thousand additional workers. Roberts had succeeded spectacularly in turning opinion around, for he was as much moved by the traditions of the works as by the spirit of the men. The chief engineer's device for measuring Brunel's original 7ft-wide lines hung in the conference room, along with a similar device for measuring the new 4ft 8½in standard gauge. That was the way Roberts liked things to be, and he always insisted that anything relevant to the GWR era that was uncovered in the works should immediately be brought to his attention.

The final Hunslet locomotives built at Swindon Works for Kenya Railways were delivered in record time – just as the first loco Great Western had been in 1846. (Andy Binks, The Swindon Society)

The renewed feeling of optimism that accompanied the turnaround in the fortunes of the Swindon Railway Works continued to contrast sharply with what was happening at many of the other manufacturing concerns in and around Swindon during 1977. Garrards, the long-established electrical components firm in the centre of the town, announced in January that year that up to 1,200 of its workers faced the axe. Later that year, workers at its parent company Plessey Hydraulics in Cheney Manor locked out the management in a bitter fight against the imminent closure of the plant. In February it was the turn of Vickers Engineering to go public with more bad news when it announced that around 650 jobs were at risk at its South Marston factory on the outskirts of the town. For Swindon's other major employer, British Leyland, the year began with an almost continuous round of lay-offs, often due to unofficial strike action at its Pressed Steel plant in

Stratton St Margaret. Fears were being expressed that the plant could be on the brink of closure, and come April, those fears were intensified by the announcement on 19 April that the Stratton plant faced 'huge cuts'. For once, it seemed as though the railway works was sailing happily along, while all else around her appeared to be sinking.

Little did I know as I prepared for my school examinations in May 1977 that I would soon become a beneficiary of this new lease of life for Swindon Works. Having followed the EITB route into engineering, it was completely by accident that I was offered an engineering apprenticeship at the Works Training School. I had deliberately skipped over most of the advertisements for apprenticeships in the *Evening Advertiser* all through the early part of that year, thinking it just wasn't for me. Even when British Rail Engineering had sent representatives to our school to give a presentation on the merits of craft apprenticeships that they were offering, I had declined to attend. It was during the autumn of that year, having recently finished with school and having no clear idea of what I was going to do with my life, that I tended to gravitate towards engineering. It was as though some irresistible force was working against me and that I would ultimately fall down into the grimy existence that I imagined to be the hallmark of factory life. The search for a reason why I took so little interest in my future employment prospects at a time when they should have been foremost in my mind commands me to reflect upon what it was like being a teenager in the 1970s. It was an era when the industrial workplace was viewed as a hate-filled environment of continuous strikes; a place where management and unions were continually at odds. The 'one out, all out' culture had taken root in many of Britain's key industries by 1977, with workers up and down the country regularly staging lightning strikes for quite often the pettiest of reasons.

Britain's industry was continually in a state of chaos and yet I was far too busy enjoying myself even to worry about aiming for a career or continuing with my education, let alone get involved in this unappealing world of endless hostility that seemed to be the permanent condition of life inside the factory. If I'd required any further guidance, the careers advisor seemed to be a very rare species at our school, and when one did finally show up she must have felt as though she was wasting her time for my ambition never went beyond working in a fishing tackle shop. The few careers films that were shown to us at school on Friday afternoons, screened with the intention of guiding us in our career choices, were mostly grainy, black and white films from the 1960s. The outdated suits and hairstyles made the people look as though they had been lifted from a Ken Loach kitchen sink drama.[29] I remember one particular film that was shown with the intended aim of enticing people into the construction industry, along with the promise of £3 per week starting pay. There were howls of laughter throughout the lecture theatre from pupils who were already receiving such an amount in pocket money! The one and only careers film that centred on engineering that I can remember presented an image of the trade that corresponded with how I'd imagined it to be, an occupation in which you were forever covered in oil and grease and would spend half of your life filing metal. In all honesty, this fuzzy, black and white representation that was screened wasn't too far removed from the modern world, for there were no Computer Numerical Control (CNC) machines to impress you, and digital displays on conventional machines were still quite a rare thing. There were no personal computers and some engineers were still using slide rules and log tables to calculate measurements. If you went down the town on a Saturday afternoon, the most impressive piece of hi-tech equipment you could buy was a scientific pocket calculator (finally small enough to fit in your pocket) for about £17.[30] This device would make trigonometry easy for you by calling up sines, cosines and tangents at the touch of a button, a marvellous gadget for an engineer to own in 1977!

Forty-odd years on, we now live in a world where people have grown dependent on technology that would have been unimaginable back in 1977. Today, the vast majority of people are either locked into social media or scrutinising data uploads throughout almost every waking hour. We would at once feel as though we had lost our connection to the world if we were deprived of our smartphones or other hi-tech gadgets, this despite the fact that we had actually enjoyed living in a world devoid of such technology. I and my colleagues of a similar age continue to this day to reminisce about how brilliant life had been back in the 1970s. It wasn't just the gloriously hot summers with long months of cloudless skies either. In 1977 it was a fantastic time to be a 16-year-old. For many local people, the year was embellished by the many street parties arranged in celebration of the Queen's Silver Jubilee in June of that year. Two hundred and thirty streets throughout Swindon were officially closed to traffic, and there was a huge commotion in Beatrice Street when a whole pig being roasted for the occasion suddenly burst into flames.[31] As for us teenagers, we were celebrating the Jubilee in our own way – getting into the raw energy of the Sex Pistols and their banned song 'God Save the Queen'.

Up to that point, the big night of the week had always been Wednesdays and the teenage disco at the Brunel Rooms in The Parade. *Saturday Night Fever* had recently been doing the rounds and 40p would get you in among all of the other John Travolta impersonators. Now the grotesque flared trousers, 'tank-tops' and platform-heeled shoes of the Glam Rock era had given way to the spiky, coloured hair and bulldog clips associated with the age of punk rock. There were so many exciting new bands coming along; it seemed as though there was a new one every week – The Stranglers, The Clash, The Jam, Blondie, Elvis Costello and the Attractions, Ian Dury and the Blockheads – I think virtually all of my wages for the first two years of my apprenticeship was spent watching bands!

The town's football team has always held a special place in the heart of most Swindonians, railwaymen in particular who would have made up the large majority of spectators during the early years of the club. Even Harold J. Fleming, arguably the greatest player ever to wear a Swindon Town shirt, went inside the GWR Works as a young lad, before turning professional in 1908 on £4 a week.[32] If one discounts the hooligan element that blighted the game for much of the 1970s, watching football was definitely better. Before the insistence upon all-seater stadiums following the Hillsborough tragedy, thousands would cram onto the Town End terraces on a Saturday afternoon to watch mostly home-grown players giving it their all for Swindon Town F.C. The football club was emphatically adding to that feelgood factor in 1977 when the team went on one of its famous cup runs. In January of that year Swindon defeated a Fulham side, containing such greats as George Best, Rodney Marsh and Bobby Moore, 5-0 at the County Ground, and was rewarded with a home tie against the mighty Everton later that month. Despite the howls of protest from many disgruntled fans complaining about the £1 admission fee, they turned up in their thousands to watch a highly entertaining 2-2 draw. The Town were ultimately beaten 2-1 in the replay at Goodison Park.

Away from football, much of my spare time during the summer of 1977 was spent at the town's favourite fishing spot at Coate Water Country Park, where throughout the previous couple of years the park had to be closed to fisherman for long periods when thousands of fish had died from a mystery disease. In April 1975, 8 tons of fish had been taken away by the lorry-load and discarded, while baffled scientific experts worked around the clock as they sought to arrive at a diagnosis. Those of us who regularly enjoyed our fishing at Coate Water had begun to wonder if there were any fish left in the lake.

This was Swindon in 1977, and whilst being somewhat unashamedly immersed in this carefree utopia, I should have been remembering that sound piece of advice my father had given to me about, 'Not ending up in a bloody factory'. I knew for sure that I didn't want to go back to Dorcan Comprehensive School to study for A-levels. At that time, Dorcan was Swindon's newest and largest school of that type, and I have to confess that I never put in the necessary effort to make a success of my secondary education. For whatever reason, during the years that mattered I clearly lacked the motivation to try and do well, this despite the fact that there were some very good teachers at Dorcan back in the 1970s who, without me realising it at the time, influenced me significantly. Also, aside from my clear lack of motivation and downright laziness, there were others in my year who were successful, who did get into university – Oxford and Cambridge included! When I exited the school gates for the last time in May 1977 I was walking away from a five-year period during which I had achieved almost total academic failure at this all-modern school that had been very rich in facilities. I left Dorcan with an assortment of nine Certificate of Secondary Education passes. My one solitary Grade One pass in art has a certain significance attached to it, owing to the fact that a few years down the track I would ultimately be apprenticed to painting!

On the day I filled out the application for that apprenticeship, I had applied half-heartedly beneath the illusion that if I got myself a trade then I would be set up for life. I was forever being told by those around me that getting a trade would be the best route to follow. Considering how disinterested and uninspired I was at the time, I have to concede that, having previously missed the apprenticeship boat so to speak, I was exceedingly lucky when my one and only application for an engineering apprenticeship turned out to be successful.

Having applied, I was always mindful that the company with whom this first year was undertaken was not committed to sponsoring the remainder of the apprenticeship. This would only happen if the trainee did well in that first year, which meant the selection procedure was particularly tough as applicants would be judged according to whether they came across as being a good or bad investment risk. I remember having to attend the first stage of the process at a place called the Burkhardt Hall, a large, red brick Victorian building situated alongside the Regent Circus Technical College, in the late summer of 1977. The session began with a series of puzzles in what was deemed to be an aptitude test. Typical problems to be solved were of the kind 'If you turn cog A clockwise, which direction would cog E turn'? If you were successful at solving these types of 'problems' you were then invited for a formal interview inside the main college building, which turned out to be a far more unpleasant experience than the solving of a few brain-teasers. Each candidate was called up before a four-strong, heavy-smoking selection panel, consisting of two EITB representatives and two men strongly allied in some way to engineering trade unions. I remember feeling very intimidated by the whole thing and that the two union men seemed far more interested in my father's employment and also the general attitude within my household in respect of the trade-union movement as a whole, which was very powerful at around that time. The first question they asked was 'where did my father work and was the company where he worked unionised?' When I answered in the negative, I remember being scrutinised with a long, cold stare over the tops of the spectacles worn by the two astonished union representatives. Here I was, a wet behind the ears 16-year-old at his first job interview being interrogated about my father's non-union membership! Such an occurrence today would probably be seized upon by the tabloid newspapers as a national scandal!

Thereafter, my prospects of being selected did not really improve much when the EITB representative began making enquiries regarding the kind of things that I had been reading in the papers lately. 'What aspects of the news have caught your eye recently Ron,' he asked, and endeavoured to prompt me to think about current affairs – the ongoing pay caps enacted by the Callaghan-led Labour government and the resulting industrial action – that sort of thing. Somewhat bewildered by this line of questioning, I sat and thought about this for about thirty seconds before replying, 'I don't know really, I can only remember reading about Geoffrey Boycott scoring his one hundredth first-class century against the Australians at Headingley.'[33]

The selection panel were struck dumb by this response. Their display of face-pulling and sideways glances seemed to convey a united opinion that they were wasting their time and the board's money on me. As they stubbed out their cigarettes in unison, I could sense that they had deduced from this absurd interaction that I certainly wasn't 'convenor material', or would not be of any use to 'the Movement' whatsoever.[34] And yet, regardless of my juvenile innocence, I must have succeeded in making some sort of favourable impression upon them, for I was in due course offered a place as a first-year apprentice, and thankfully, I never in the course of my training schedule set eyes on any of my four interrogators again!

I often think that if I had taken the more direct route into the school via BREL I might have found the entry test a little easier. Technical apprentice Keith Shailes (1977 intake) remembers no such similar interrogation:

> When I left school in the summer of 1977, there was only ever going to be one career for me. My dad was an electrician at Garrards in the town, and the natural choice was an apprenticeship. He'd have loved me to join him at Garrards, but the offer came from British Rail, having passed the test of 'how to repair a bicycle puncture'. At the time, there were a number of industries in the town that used the facilities of the BR Works Training School, so I would have ended up there whether Garrards or British Rail had offered me my opportunity.

No doubt the entry process was a bit more difficult than Keith makes it sound, (and his dad did eventually join him at the Swindon Works for its final few years). For other wannabe apprentices, the entry tests took a different turn, as vehicle builder Keith Miller (1975 intake) remembers:

> I had to read a piece from an engineering book about using engineer's blue to find high spots, etc. The interviewer (Roy Hazell) then asked questions about the aforementioned passage. I guess this was to gauge if you could grasp the principle of what you had just read.

The entry test for outstation apprentice David Vaughan (1975 intake) was similar. However, at his initial interview at Western Tower in Reading his strategy of total honesty turned out to have been the best policy:

> I had the initial interview at Western Tower. I was asked how a lighting circuit worked, then what DMU stood for, followed by what EMU stood for and the difference between the two. I remember my dad (fitter Billy Vaughan from Reading depot) cringing when I didn't have a clue and told the interviewer I wasn't interested in trains and just wanted an electrical apprenticeship. Later I remember reading a passage about a lathe and Roy Hazell asking me questions about what I had read to determine if I had taken everything on board.

As for successful EITB applicants such as me, there was an equal chance of being sent to either one of British Rail Engineering Ltd, the Royal Military College of Science or the doomed Vickers Engineering facility in South Marston to complete the first year of training. It was around three weeks after my interview that I received that big, buff-coloured envelope requesting me to report myself to the British Rail Works Training School. My earlier relief that school was finally over and done with, and my enjoyment of the long hot summer we had long been in the grip of, evaporated in an instant. I was going back to school again, and yet, little did I realise that this time it would be to a very different kind of school. This was a school where everyone who attended was made to feel important, for the simple reason that he or she would be carrying on the tradition that had put Swindon on the map. The doors to that flagship training school, where all the railway apprentices in the Western Region were prepared for their first taste of factory life, were flung open for me. Despite the negative comments from others alluding to the precarious state of the works, my parents did indeed congratulate me as though I had won some sort of coveted prize. Later that morning I sat and read slowly through the prospectus that accompanied the letter of acceptance; the only thing I remember was that, as I closed the final page of the booklet, I didn't feel much like celebrating!

2

THE WORKS TRAINING SCHOOL

I have always been of the firm opinion that no engineering apprentice ever fared better in the first year of his or her training than those who attended the Swindon Works Training School. The most important thing about the school was that right from your very first hour as a trainee you were made to feel special. There was never any mention of the fact that the works had been rescued from the jaws of doom and was still effectively fighting for its future. It was impressed upon all of us railway apprentices from the very start that we were carrying on a very important and long-standing tradition. It was a tradition that at that time did not really mean an awful lot to me – probably owing to the fact that nobody in my own family had ever been inside Swindon Works.

The school I was about to attend on that first morning was originally authorised by the British Transport Commission on 21 November 1957. Its construction formed part of a £1.2 billion programme for modernising Britain's ageing railways.[35] The training schools for each of the main works – Swindon, Derby, Doncaster, Crewe, Eastleigh, Horwich, Springburn, Stratford, York and Wolverton – were intended to form a key part of that strategy. Their conception represented a whole new approach to the process of training apprentices, the idea being that the trainee could be steered towards the trade for which he or she was deemed to be best suited. There was an additional element of tradition in play here, as during the early days of the GWR the apprentices were always required to make their own tools. The continuation of this tradition was reflected in the test pieces that apprentices had to make as they worked their way around the various sections. We were required to make scribing blocks, die stocks, toolboxes and even a stool, complete with a neatly trimmed cushion. It was also a stated aim of the curriculum to make the lad into a 'good citizen' as well as a good craftsman – an aim that to their credit I believe they were generally very successful in achieving.

Having been designed to cover an area of over 11,000 sq ft, the school had been equipped from the outset with an impressive machine shop, which in my time boasted eighteen Harrison centre lathes, two Colchester lathes, two Ward lathes and at least four universal milling machines. There was also a sheet metal/fabrication workshop, electrical engineering workshops, a carpentry area, a welding bay and two fitting workshops. Also, during my time at the school an assembly room, a gymnasium and lecture rooms were provided, but I'm told that these facilities were later utilised for other purposes. The school was designed to cater for somewhere around 100 apprentices for only their first year of training. It was officially opened on 25 April 1963, but had actually commenced training operations much earlier on 17 September 1962.[36] By 1970, the school had begun to accept first-year apprentices from other engineering companies around the Swindon area, including Plessey Semi-Conductors, Square D and Garrard Engineering.

The theory component of much of the apprentice training was ultimately transferred to the Swindon College sites at Regent Circus and North Star Avenue. Because the school served the whole of the Western Region, there were a number of outstation apprentices from depots in Bristol, Reading, Cardiff, Greater London, Exeter and Plymouth. Outstation apprentices were based at a three-floor hostel in Bath Road with accommodation for twenty-seven apprentices.

I had never before laid eyes on the Works Training School, nor was I remotely familiar with the area where it was situated. On my very first day when my father dropped me at the entrance to Dean Street on a chilly, late summer morning, I ventured forth apprehensively, all the time wondering what the hell I was letting myself in for. I remember when I was about halfway up Dean Street I took a sideways glance through the window of a terraced house, where I espied a large dog sprawled upon a rug in front of an open fire. People had earlier told me that factory life was a 'dog's life' and I remember thinking as I studied the slumbering mutt that dogs don't really do so badly. It

Training Officer Ken Dann with Romanian Ambassador Vasili Gliga on a tour of the Training School. (Roy Hazell Collection)

was probably the earliest time I had been out of bed for about four months, and I positively longed to be dozing in front of an open fire. I continued on until I finally sighted the school at the far end of Dean Street at the junction of Newburn Crescent, I remember feeling pleasantly surprised by the sight of the very modern-looking facility where I was to spend the next twelve months.

Upon reaching the building I entered (incorrectly) through the front door into the carpeted reception area, knowing that this would probably be the only time I would ever be allowed to do so. I had expected to find others waiting, but as I wandered around the corridors, the building appeared to be completely deserted. A rather unpleasant smell hung in the air, which I remember as being a combination of disinfectant and paraffin. I eventually veered left and at last espied a handful of sullen-looking individuals sat in the cloakroom sporting green overalls – 'greenbacks' as they would be referred to when they finally went inside. I approached the nearest lad and asked in the friendliest way possible if he was a new starter, to which, he looked at me with a stupid grin and carried on staring at the floor. Undeterred, I finally recognised a lad I had sat opposite during my aptitude test who informed me that because we were EITB-sponsored apprentices we were starting a few days later than the others, (those 'others', I soon discovered, had already had their induction). Standing around waiting to be detailed to whatever department we were to commence our training, I quickly stole a glimpse through the big double doors leading to the main workshop. I must concede here, that, aside from the powerful smell of paraffin, the machine shop did appear tremendously impressive. The workshop was deserted, and the twenty-odd centre lathes were standing motionless like abandoned artillery installations ready to do battle when the battalion returned. These were flanked by the four universal milling machines, along with a selection of surface grinders and bar-cutting machines of all sizes. What amazed me was how tidy and spotlessly clean everything was. There was not a shred of metal shavings in evidence anywhere in the shop, and a clean, graffiti-less, wooden bench accompanied every single one of the pristine-looking machines.

As there appeared to be nobody in authority anywhere in the building, we stood around chatting and getting to know each other for around half an hour. It was apparent that a large number of the lads who began their apprenticeship at the Works Training School alongside me on that first morning were also EITB-sponsored apprentices, and were as unfamiliar with the Swindon Works as I was. Not so the British Rail-sponsored apprentices. For a good number of them it was as though they were fulfilling the next stage of a predestined life pattern. Their fathers, just like their grandfathers before them, had spent their working lives inside the Swindon Works. It often seemed to me as though almost everyone who I came into contact with, either at the Training School or during our time inside the works, could boast a father, an uncle, a brother or a cousin – in fact, anything up to seven or eight other family members – who either were, or who had at one time been employed inside in one of the many railway workshops. I have no doubt that if the workshops had remained open for another hundred or so years, then their own sons and grandsons would probably be following the same destiny.

When, at last, all the induction formalities had been attended to we were then introduced to a Mr Baker, who was then the Acting Training School Manager – a tall, balding man with a beard who turned out to be a very firm, but likable man. Vic Baker welcomed us all to the school warmly with

The Works Training School Machining Section. The floor and benches were required to be spotless before the apprentices were allowed to vacate the section. (Roy Hazell Collection)

a friendly smile, and articulated a few of the not so obvious dos and don'ts in a direct yet eloquent manner that effectively held us in a temporary trance. I was soon awoken from this hypnosis when I suddenly heard him speak my name – Bateman! I signalled apprehensively, and he responded by handing me a small sheet of yellow paper, upon which he had scribbled 'Turning – B2'.

It is more shocking than funny now when I suddenly remember that, at the time, I wasn't really sure of what 'turning' actually was; in fact, I had not the slightest idea! Fortunately, a very lively and enthusiastic instructor was about to enlighten me.

'I've been 'ere for many years now since the school opened in 1962, an' I 'avn't 'ad a lad lose a finger yet,' bragged the feisty sixty-something to whom I had been allocated as he drew his opening address to a close. I certainly wouldn't imply that this rather elderly man in the starched white overall was really a braggart, for he was in all sincerity a very effective and dedicated instructor. Jack Bevan was a short, slim-built man with thinning white hair and largish ears. Although he was past 60, and probably among the oldest of the instructors, he was as sharp as a tack, in the sense that he missed absolutely nothing. This sprightly looking old fellow had been saddled with umpteen yobbish-looking school leavers, lads who might well have been an impossible mixture of punk rockers, bikers and possible football hooligans, yet he went about his vocation confidently. He judged nobody by their looks, and his fatherly style of explanation seemed to get the message through even the thickest of skulls. Mr Bevan was also a stickler for cleanliness and preached safety eight hours a day.

Additional assistance in the machine shop was on offer in the form of a much less dynamic fellow of around fifty-something with thin, dark hair swept comb-over-style across his balding crown. The assistant was intolerably slow throughout his demonstrations – once he had your attention you could not get rid of him for what seemed like hours. The lads were expected to complete a set number of tasks on each section during a six-week period and almost inevitably some, not necessarily healthy, competition had developed between us as though it were a kind of race. A session with the assistant instructor was a far from welcome interruption if you wanted to stay ahead, or even try to keep up with the field.

The section belonged to Mr Bevan, the older and more dynamic of the two instructors, and whose presence dominated every workspace and walkway. In between instructing the apprentices, he was required to keep going backwards and forwards to the grinding wheels to sharpen various tools, as well as feed material into the bar cutter. When on the section, it often seemed as though there were too many lads making too many mistakes for him to keep on top of. He seemed to be forever hot-footing it from one machine to another saying, 'Shut off yer machine son, shut off yer machine.' His method incorporated a repertoire of commands that would pierce the drone of the twenty-odd turning machines, however vigorously the spindles were rotating. Always ten minutes prior to finishing the session, his sharp command would rip clearly through the din of the machinery, 'Last cuts lads!' And thereafter, the heavy drone of the countless rotating spindles would gradually fade to a gentle hum from the motors of one or two stragglers finishing off cuts. The cleaning process and the additional preparations for vacating the section would then proceed with military precision at a pace, with our instructor Mr Bevan as the Supreme Commander of Operations. Two apprentices would immediately be detailed to swarf-shovelling duty in accordance with the rota, and would stand at the head of the gangway, each holding their shovel at the ready like a pikestaff. Out would come the brooms and another four lads would sweep clean their allotted aisles, again in accordance with the rota. Thereafter, the shop floor took on the appearance of a parade ground, and with the sharpness of a drill instructor, Mr Bevan would stand stiffly between the tool cupboards demanding the return of the missing tools '… ONE 6in rule … ONE callipers … ONE centre punch …' etc. If you slacked, he would often bellow. 'Come on lads, come on, you don't get twenty-six pounds and fifty-five pence a week for nothing!'[37]

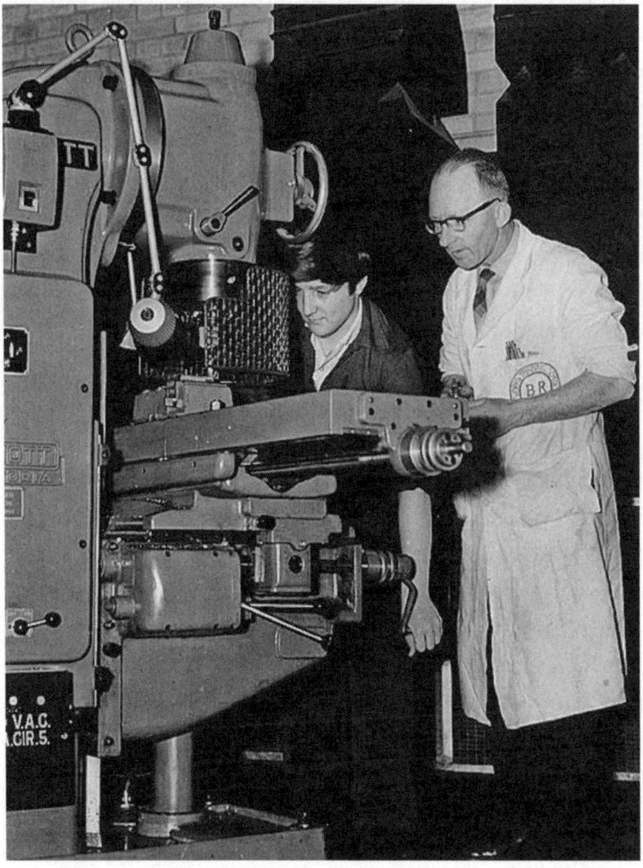

Jack Bevan instructing an apprentice in the art of horizontal milling. (Roy Hazell Collection)

One thing I can say without question is that this particular instructor's firm though friendly manner won the respect and admiration of every single one of those hundred-odd apprentices. I'll never forget on our last day at the training school, during the end-of-year presentations, when the manager of the school announced that our machine-shop instructor would be retiring next year. He was invited onto the stage to address the apprentices, after which a huge round of applause quickly turned to cheers, which then turned into a chorus of 'for he's a jolly good fellow'. It really touched the old fellow to tears to see that he had made such a good impression upon his charges.

My first experience of turning and milling had resulted in a very enjoyable six weeks, which meant that the machine shop would be a difficult act to follow. There is definitely something fascinating about turning metal bar when you first try it. I remember getting an almighty rocket for reaming out mild steel at 1,500rpm, and when on horizontal milling, picking up a large cylindrical cutter with my bare hands, then opening my palm to reveal half a dozen equally spaced cuts, oozing blood. I would have been happy to stay in the machine shop for my whole year, for it seemed better to watch a machine doing the work rather than doing the work with your own hands, as was the case with the next task that awaited me when my time in the machine shop finally came to an end.

The fitting section was next on my list, and from what I had seen it consisted of four long rows of lads doing nothing but filing metal from morning until night. This corresponded more closely with how I had always imagined a future in engineering to be. It was certainly the most boring six weeks of my time in the training school – possibly my life! We would stand there filing steel surfaces from morning till night, occasionally rubbing the surface of our work upon the 'bluing table' to check for high spots. It was incredibly tedious work, as Peter Morgan remembers, 'I struggled to understand why I stood at a workbench for weeks at a time, using a variety of files to make a piece of metal flat when there was a machine not 20ft away that could do it better in a matter of seconds.'

Quite often while filing we would make up stupid songs or hum silly tunes in unison, particularly loudly when the instructor went off the section, which was quite often in the case of our particular instructor. The lads soon began to swap theories regarding what they thought he kept nipping outside for. On the subject of our fitting instructor, I'm not so sure if I had been more than fortunate here, for there were two fitting sections, each run by two separate instructors. Our overseer was a quiet, nervous-looking man, while the instructor on the other fitting section was the complete opposite. We used to joke that had he taken on a career in acting, he could probably have slipped into the role of Kommandant very easily. On one occasion, when our own instructor had failed to show up, he entered our workshop and made us all stand in a neat semicircle around a bench. 'I've been watching you lot,' he said with a face like thunder, 'And I'm only gonna say this once. When you use a bastard file, you don't just 'old it rigid, you 'ave to old it BLOODY RIGID!' With that he threw the file onto the bench and wandered off. Sometimes at the end of the day he would make all the apprentices stand in a circular queue all around the edge of the hall, then before the clock ticked over he would make us march around the hall in a circle. After several circuits he would point to the door and out we would go. I never really knew him as I was never on his section, but I do think he quite enjoyed being an instructor. For him, a high level of discipline helped to maintain a high standard of workmanship. There was some additional good in him, for he was very knowledgeable on the subject of internal combustion engines. Often he would go to great lengths to pass on some of his very useful knowledge to the lads who had recently acquired motorcycles. Aside from those rare demonstrations of know-how, I think the lads found him a bit too unpredictable for comfort. Ade Adams probably got to know him better than most: 'I remember him telling us about when he worked on Spitfires in the RAF. He was great when you got him talking, and an alright bloke as long as you didn't cross him.'

Throughout the next three to four months I was to spend six weeks at a stretch on the electrical section, three weeks on welding, three weeks on sheet metal and fabrication and six weeks divided between carpentry and trimming. One electrical section was dedicated to teaching such skills as winding coils, while the other showed us how to bend conduit and wire basic circuits. I particularly enjoyed the sheet metal section, where we learned how to form objects, mainly by bending and shaping thin-gauge sheet metal. We were taught such skills as riveting and soldering, and also shown how to use bending and folding machines, as well as fly presses. Each apprentice emerged from the section at the end of his three weeks with a very smart toolbox (complete with tray) that was all his (or her) very own work. I say 'her' because being the late

Apprentices receive instruction in electrical circuitry at the Works Training School. (Roy Hazell Collection)

1970s, very much on the wave of the equal rights for women campaign, the British Rail Training School had begun accepting its first female engineering apprentices. Christine Bogdaniec and Vanessa Street became the first in 1975, followed by Valerie Nicholas a year later. Christine thoroughly enjoyed her time at the WTS and forwarded her own recollection forty-four years later:

> Myself and Vanessa were the first two ladies to enter the school. We settled in well and the boys looked after us. The instructors did initially wrap us in cotton wool, but we soon became 'one of the lads', and were treated accordingly. I do remember one instructor saying to me in my final week that I had a choice to do nothing, or he would teach us about two- or four-stroke engines – I chose the latter! I have very fond memories of both the apprentices, and the instructors. Not forgetting then kitchen staff, who made a mean cheese sandwich.

Sixteen-year-old technical apprentice Yvonne Bradshaw entered the school in the 1977 intake, and was surprised to discover she was the only female among 100 boys!

> I had arrived at the school on my first day expecting to be with a small minority of girls. However, I was to be the only girl amongst a hundred boys, which was a daunting prospect for a 16-year-old girl. I remember walking into the assembly hall full of would-be male apprentices all talking wildly. Slowly everyone stopped talking until there was silence with a hundred boys staring at me.
>
> At first it was a lonely working life with workmates afraid to talk to me. It must be remembered that up until the late seventies women's working roles had been teachers, nurses or secretaries. Now with women working in engineering, that was something different that the workforce and the workplace had to deal with. After a few months of getting used to me I was treated as one of the boys. I was even given the nickname of 'Reg' so I would fit in. I was at a major disadvantage compared to the boys because in those days schools only allowed girls to learn cookery and sewing, not woodwork or metalwork. My manual skills were sadly lacking against the beautiful craftwork of the boys. However, everybody recognised the difficulties of my disadvantage and offered encouragement for me to keep improving.

I was also surprised to discover that in amongst all this practical training, we were all allocated an hour each week for physical education. I imagined this would involve some circuit training or jogging, or some other form of physical exertion to keep all the apprentices fit. When we turned up at the gym expecting to meet our 'drill instructor', we were met by a young lad from the works holding a football. 'It's a nice day outside,' he began, 'So let us all go over to the park and have a nice game of football.' And that is how it continued, week in, week out. Some of the lads saw this as an opportunity to smoke for an hour, while only paying lip service to the game in progress. When it rained, we stayed inside the school gym and played a strange game called crab football, which is basically playing football while sat on the gymnasium floor. It was strange to see grown lads sliding over the floor on their backsides trying to kick a football, but it was all good fun!

At around the time that the six weeks about on the various sections was coming to a close it was discovered that, owing to changes in forthcoming workloads, British Rail Engineering was going to suffer a severe shortage of vehicle body finishers and painters. EITB apprentices were invited to apply to be taken on by British Rail Engineering, and upon application for a job as a vehicle body finisher I was told that 'vehicle painting' was all they could offer. I thought about it for a couple of hours and eventually, very reluctantly I might add, accepted the offer. It was a permanent, seemingly well-paid job, and that was all there was to it. At that time there was still no guarantee that I would be taken on as a turner elsewhere to continue my apprenticeship, so I thought, 'Well as least I will finally get my hands on a real wage packet, as opposed to a pink EITB cheque for nineteen quid every week.'

As it turned out, I would still have another six months of pink EITB cheques before I finally got that coveted wage packet. Six months of instruction in the art of vehicle painting, a trade for which the Works Training School was at that time hopelessly ill-equipped to offer. To everyone's knowledge, no apprentice painters had been trained in the school for at least the last ten years. Previous painting apprentices had been sent outstation to learn certain aspects of their trade. A kindly, middle-aged man was recruited from among the skilled painters in the workshops to be our new instructor. The man they chose introduced himself as Ron Clack; he was close on 60, a likeable fellow who was probably chosen on account of his signwriting and French polishing experience, and not forgetting his sound knowledge of first aid. When we began our training, we soon discovered that the painting apprentices were to be lumped in with the trimming apprentices, and because no painters or trimmers had been trained for donkey's years, it was also discovered that the school possessed little or no painting or trimming materials to speak of. The painting and trimming section consisted of two workbenches and three empty cupboards.

Ron Clack refused to be fazed by the almost total unpreparedness of the school to be able to fulfil the task of training three new apprentice painters. Armed with a selection of age-old craft manuals, our instructor set about acquiring all the materials needed to teach us the rudiments of applying a good coat of paint, coupled with a variety of near obsolete skills intended to keep things interesting. The usefulness of some of these skills, such as wood graining, gilding and lining, had long since vanished elsewhere, but definitely not inside those railway workshops. Having said that, it was amusing, and often quite interesting, to discover these skills and try our hand at them. I think the three of us who trained as painters at the time appreciated the lengths that Ron went to on our behalf, intent on seeing to it that we received a decent level of training. He knew that when we entered the workshops proper we would immediately discover that the painters were as proud a collection of men as any other tradesmen within the workshops. He merely wanted to make us aware that any lapses in workmanship that could affect the reputation of 'the gang' would not be tolerated. As things turned out, we spent most of our time employed in carrying out decorating work and other essential maintenance tasks to the Training School building. All the walls were given a fresh coat of emulsion, and all the coat pegs and lockers were neatly signwritten by the time we left the school. There was also a steady stream of apprentices who wanted the toolboxes they had made on the sheet metal section painted up to stop them from rusting. It wasn't long before the fuel tanks from their motorcycles began to appear with special instructions for colour schemes and outrageous designs.

So, despite the fact that neither of the three of us painters had ever had any desire to be painters, we had taken it on because there would be no other options open to us if we wanted to work for British Rail. In the years that followed, many apprentices chose to be painters for a variety of reasons and Ron Clack continued in the role of instructor, after having had a very successful first year with us lot! I got to work with Ron occasionally inside the works proper, and seeing as he was a man of high moral fibre, nobody ever swore in front of him – which was a rare thing in Swindon Works. The limit of Ron's curses amounted to 'flipping heck' and I noticed reading through the comments of other painters that this had rubbed off on the apprentice painters that came along after us. Bob Skinner of the 1978 intake was drawn towards the trade by the mixture of useful skills.

> I opted to become a painter as there seemed to be more variety to what we would learn, i.e. painting, French polishing, signwriting, building maintenance and paint-spraying at the college. During our first year at the Training School we were on trestles painting the classroom walls under the watchful eye of dear old 'flipping heck' Ron Clack.

For Paul Armstrong, also from the 1978 intake, it was an easier decision, but being a painter inside Swindon Works turned out to be not quite what he expected:

> I remember starting out trying my hand at all the trades on offer at the Works Training School. As we got closer to decision day I gravitated towards painting. My older brother was a paint-sprayer at Bampton-Brothers in Swindon. I loved cars and thought I would follow him into the trade. At the time I assumed we would have done more spraying. Aside from when we were on day-release at the college, the only spraying we did was the carriage lamps in an ante room off of the Spring Shop.

Whilst attending the Work's Training School, and right throughout our four-year apprenticeship, we were required to attend the North Star Technical College for one and a half days each week for technical instruction. It was called North Star after Brunel's famous broad-gauge engine, presumably because the college had been built on former railway works land. I always look back upon those days with mixed memories, some quite humorous and others of what it felt like to be unpopular. The reason that we were unpopular was because, to put it bluntly, we were a rough-looking lot compared to the other students at the college, and the last thing the college staff wanted was gangs of youths – some looking much like typical 1970s hooligans – marauding around the corridors of their establishment, which I believe is how two-thirds of us were regarded. I say two-thirds, because a third of the apprentices who attended college (the 'C' group) were referred to as technical apprentices. They were working towards much higher qualifications, and were far more dedicated towards achieving their academic goals.

As one of the non-technical apprentices, I would have to admit that the behaviour of our group (group 'B') was far from exemplary, and I believe this had something to do with our feelings of being let off the leash for a day and a half. As we saw it, these lecturers at the college were not paying our wages, so while we were out of the sight of our employers, we were out to have an easy time. I'm ashamed to admit that this attitude to day release endured right throughout my apprenticeship, especially when we began going into pubs during our lunch break. At the halfway mark of that first year, we had to switch to Regent Circus College, which was surrounded by them – a pub in every direction! I also soon learned that no apprentice ever got sacked for failing any examinations and, come to think of it, the prize for passing an examination was a mere fiver.

Looking back, I think my attitude to the technical aspects in the later years of my apprenticeship was poor mainly because the things we were learning at college bore no relation to what it was like learning a trade inside the works – especially brush-painting railway carriages. When doubts about the future of the works came up for discussion, and even the lecturers at the college were asking us if we thought British Rail would close us down, we got to thinking, 'What did it matter if one never attained the qualifications for what looked set to become an obsolete trade anyhow?'

As a first-year apprentice, I seem to remember getting off on the right foot, arriving at the college on time with a smart folder, all the notes neatly written up, headings underlined, etc. Part of the reason for things going downhill thereafter had a lot to do with the manner in which many of the classroom sessions were conducted; lecturers just seemed to wander into the class and begin setting down notes upon a blackboard for us to copy – without any introduction, or much explanation to support the notes that they were writing down. Other lecturers were content to stand chatting to apprentices about their own 'humorous' experiences across a lifetime spent in engineering – the usual factory pranks involving compressed air, etc., without ever getting down to any serious work. Some of my classmates grew wise to those lecturers that could be easily 'stalled' and would deliberately ask the kind of leading questions that would distract them from the curriculum, and the whole session would evolve towards a laugh and a chat.

> I remember an old guy called Mr Deveraux was a good laugh. He used to switch his hearing aid off when he was lecturing us so it was a waste of time trying to ask him a question. When he set us work to do and we started laughing, joking and taking the Micky, he had switched it back on and heard everything!
>
> Malcolm Miles

> One of Mr Deveraux's sayings was 'rigidity – that's what you need on your wedding night!'
>
> Chris Rees

It must be said, however, that many of the practical sessions were very interesting as we got to grips with testing metals for various properties – ductility, malleability, tensile strength, etc.

When the time came for you to be allocated a trade – which in my case was painting – your technical training would become a lot more specialised, and responsibility for your instruction would be spread between fewer instructors. A short, balding man by the name of Chippendale looked after the three of us painters – a very likeable old bloke from Bradford, who, I'm ashamed to admit, we never afforded the respect that he deserved. The college workshop set aside for painting was geared solely towards instructing students in the disciplines relevant to interior decoration – certainly not for City & Guilds Vehicle Painting: Levels One, Two and Advanced. Although similarly as ill-equipped as Ron Clack for the task in hand, our man from Bradford went out on a limb to help us all he could. He would diligently research the materials and techniques that we would need to learn to fulfil the assignments, obtaining the right textbooks that contained the theory we would have to internalise, etc., and yet, for all his pains, nine weeks out of ten all the poor man got in return was utter disinterest. Even sensing this, Mr Chippendale did everything he could to try to make the course that much more interesting for us – to the extent that we spent many weeks on designing and decorating glass panels with gilded heraldry, utilising significant amounts of real gold leaf at an enormous expense to the department.

Try as the old gentleman might to instil a spark of enthusiasm into our course, we still continued to treat our day release at the college as a day off. When we went over to the works, our day release was always on a Friday, when lunch breaks could be spent at a local club called The Affair in the Wyvern Centre, just off to the left of the old Regent Circus College. This usually involved drinking over-priced lager and watching the resident stripper going through her routine. Sometimes we would play pool at one of the many pubs situated around the periphery of the college, and then return to the classroom the worse for drink. I remember on one occasion the training officer of the railway works must have been tipped off about our shenanigans. During one typically overstretched lunch hour he sent his deputy inside The Affair while the object of our attention was midway through her performance. Trying hard to ignore the 'attraction' slowly peeling off on centre stage, he began rounding up all the apprentices to get them back into college.

In order to ensure that all apprentices attended their college lessons, each trainee was required to present to the wages clerk a chit signed by the lecturer of each lesson. For a while, this could be overcome by inserting the chit of an absent lad into the pack of chits when they were rounded up and signed off at the end of the lesson. The lecturers soon got wise to this, and thereafter began making headcounts to see if this matched up with the number of chits presented. From hereon we had to become very effective forgers to be able to bunk off lessons, and some of us were exceptionally good at this. No less so the painters, for so ill-equipped was the college for teaching vehicle painters the technical aspects of the trade that we often felt as though we were a burden they could have well done without anyhow. Most of the time we were just lumped in with the vehicle body finishers who attended college on the same day as us painters, which meant we spent many hours learning things we simply would not need to know, nor would we get questioned upon any of those aspects come exam time. Subsequently the painters were often inconspicuous by their absence – we often believed that we were doing them a favour by absenting ourselves occasionally. You might ask how on earth we passed our examinations; the simple answer is that the three of us painters couldn't possibly fail with our very good friend from Bradford, Mr Chippendale, watching our backs. While we were all out supping beer and playing pool, the old fellow would be working his socks off on our behalf to ensure that we had the best opportunity to complete our assignments to perfection. All of the academic stuff required to pass the multi-choice aspect of the exam was somehow internalised during the occasional, non-practical sessions we would spend in his classroom. When I look at my City & Guilds certificates today I'm completely baffled as to how I managed to pass my part two practical examination with distinction, especially when I think of how much old Mr Chippendale willed us through those examinations, in the same manner as a jockey frantically tries to will a flagging racehorse across the finishing line. This is because whenever I think of my college days I can only remember beer, strippers and pool tables.

During that first year at the WTS, the consecutive day-and-a-half release college sessions for the A, B and C groups would finish by Friday lunchtime – meaning the entire intake at the Training School would be present on Friday afternoons, when the focus would be very much on health and safety. Another remarkable thing to mention about the Works Training School was the absolute

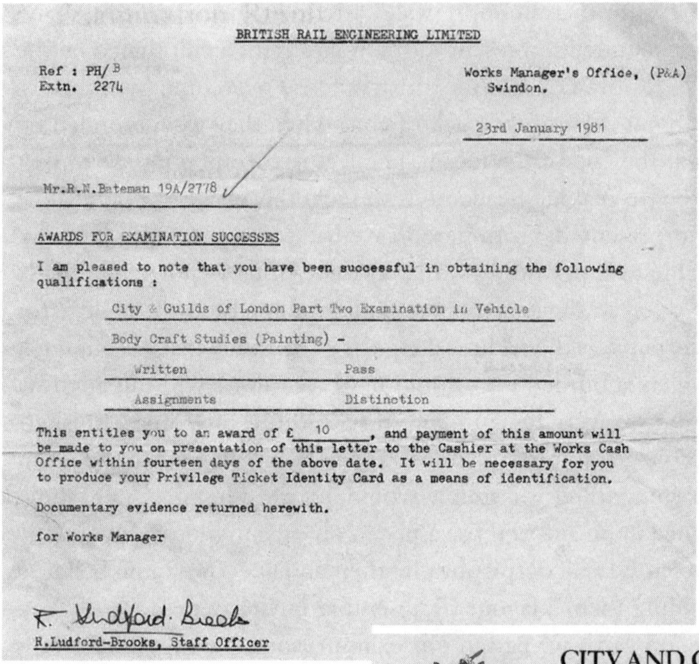

BRITISH RAIL ENGINEERING LIMITED

Ref : PH/B
Extn. 2274

Works Manager's Office, (P&A)
Swindon.

23rd January 1981

Mr.R.N.Bateman 19A/2778

AWARDS FOR EXAMINATION SUCCESSES

I am pleased to note that you have been successful in obtaining the following qualifications :

City & Guilds of London Part Two Examination in Vehicle
Body Craft Studies (Painting) -

Written	Pass
Assignments	Distinction

This entitles you to an award of £ 10 , and payment of this amount will be made to you on presentation of this letter to the Cashier at the Works Cash Office within fourteen days of the above date. It will be necessary for you to produce your Privilege Ticket Identity Card as a means of identification.

Documentary evidence returned herewith.

for Works Manager

R. Ludford-Brooks
R.Ludford-Brooks, Staff Officer

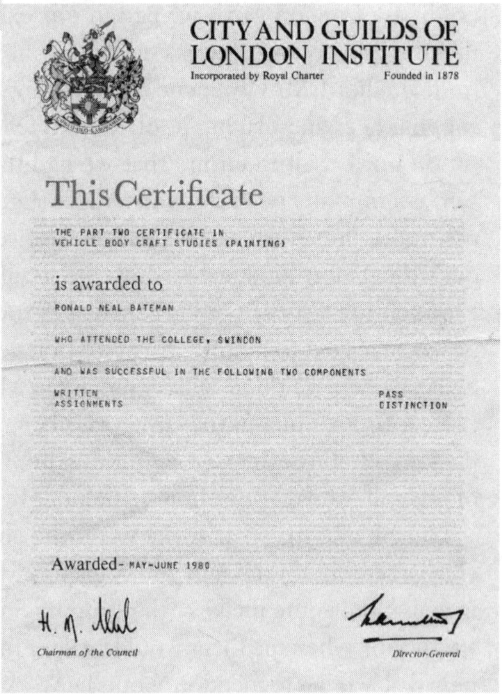

CITY AND GUILDS OF LONDON INSTITUTE
Incorporated by Royal Charter Founded in 1878

This Certificate

THE PART TWO CERTIFICATE IN
VEHICLE BODY CRAFT STUDIES (PAINTING)

is awarded to

RONALD NEAL BATEMAN

WHO ATTENDED THE COLLEGE, SWINDON

AND WAS SUCCESSFUL IN THE FOLLOWING TWO COMPONENTS

WRITTEN	PASS
ASSIGNMENTS	DISTINCTION

Awarded- MAY-JUNE 1980

Chairman of the Council

Director-General

The prize for gaining a distinction was a mere fiver – the same as for the simple pass. One did get presented with a nice certificate – or rather it turned up in the post!

dedication of the staff and instructors towards safety at work, and in particular first aid instruction. Special mention here must be afforded to the dedication of a lively and enthusiastic gentleman I remember very well. Tom Smith went beyond his duties as an instructor/coordinator in his efforts towards preparing the apprentices for adulthood to essentially steer them towards being a bit more caring and thoughtful throughout their adult life. I mentioned earlier that a stated aim of the school was to steer the apprentice towards being a good citizen, and I think Mr Smith was instrumental in achieving that. He would share with us the various enlightening incidents that occurred in the course of his own life, and pass on to us the knowledge and wisdom that only comes from experience. I feel certain that Mr Smith was highly influential in turning the raw recruits that had first entered the school twelve months earlier into a much more considerate, well-mannered, altruistic crowd. I remember when we finished for Christmas at the Training School, the last thing Tom said to us was, 'Make absolutely certain that you thank your mother for all of her hard work when you've eaten Christmas dinner – it will mean the absolute world to her.' That was the type of guy Tom was; 'good manners cost nothing' he would say over and over again. We all knew he was right, and I would like to think those 100-odd apprentices all did thank their mothers that Christmas Day!

The other three first-aid instructors took their enthusiasm from Mr Smith, and the four of them worked tirelessly to ensure that no apprentice ever left the training school without first having attained his or her first-aid badge, nor without having gained a sound appreciation of safe working procedures. To achieve this, the whole of Friday afternoons were given over to lectures and demonstrations of safety hazards, and to effective application of the current first-aid procedures. Practical instruction was given for weeks on end, with apprentices taking on the role of accident casualties. Classrooms suddenly had the appearance of overcrowded emergency rooms following a major incident. Occasionally, doctors were invited to the school on Friday afternoons to give lectures on aspects of human biology and healthy living, and also about contemporary problems such as the use of hard drugs. One such doctor, who sounded half-German, made regular visits to the school and would lecture the apprentices on past cases that he had been involved with. He had an unusually loud voice, and almost every case example that he presented to us seemed to end with the words '… and then he died'. It was no surprise that the lads came to refer to him as Doctor Death!

First-aid instruction was a key element of every apprentice's year at the Works Training School. (Roy Hazell Collection)

The high emphasis on first aid seemed to run nationwide throughout the whole network of British Rail's engineering workshops. Regional competitions were held where mock accidents or other major incidents were staged, and teams from all over the country were judged according to how effectively they responded and applied treatment to the casualties. Swindon had a great reputation for excellence in first aid and had won the regional competition on many occasions. Most apprentices were won over by this long tradition, and carried on their dedication to keeping up to date with first-aid procedures right through the remaining years of their apprenticeship and beyond, and there were good incentives offered by British Rail to continue to do this. Every year that you passed your first-aid exam you were awarded an extra day's holiday, plus an extra free railway pass. If you attended the refresher course of four one-and-a-half-hour sessions during work time and then went on to pass the exam, you were awarded two extra days holiday and two extra free railway passes.

At the end of the Training School year there were competitions to be entered and awards to be presented. The most prestigious of these was the Apprentice of the Year award, which was presented to the person who performed best overall in all disciplines during their first year's training. The winner's name would be engraved upon a huge shield that was displayed in the upstairs foyer. There were also awards presented to those apprentices who had excelled in aspects of college work and practical skills, and to those who had attained the best marks in their end-of-year examinations. I also remember the training officer took great delight in revealing one particular set of statistics – how many sandwiches, Chelsea buns and doughnuts that the apprentices had consumed throughout the course of their year at the school. There was rarely such a thing as healthy eating advice back in 1977, meaning the apprentices would be stuffed so full of sugary cakes and carbonated drinks I wouldn't be surprised if half of them were chewing with false teeth by now.

The one final task before our leaving the school was for us to sign the indentures relevant to the trade to which we were being apprenticed. Our fathers were invited to the school to witness these proceedings and to ask any questions. The short interview was also accompanied by a general overview of the apprentice's performance throughout the passing year. When my turn came around, the acting manager of the school looked me up and down and said to my father, 'I hardly know what to say, I suppose he's been one of the quiet ones; not made much of an impression while he's been with us, which I suppose is a good thing, as most of them make an impression for all the wrong reasons.' Thinking about my conduct on occasions during college day release (outlined above), it would not be long before I began to make an impression among the training staff for all the wrong reasons.

On our final afternoon at the Works Training School, in line with tradition, the then Works Manager Harry Roberts was invited to address the apprentices who were about to enter the workshops proper. I remember being particularly touched by the very high regard in which Mr Roberts was held by the staff at the school, and the level of respect afforded to him. I was completely unaware during my time at the works that he was a decorated war hero, having been wounded and subsequently captured during the Battel of Arnhem in 1944.[38] There was an air of warmth and sincerity about him that appealed to me, and I felt a great feeling of respect towards him, even though I barely knew him. He made it clear to all of us new apprentices that we were coming over to the works to join him – thereby creating the impression that we were all on the same team – and this at a time when the term 'teamwork' had rarely been coined in an industrial sense. I also remember Mr Roberts taking this

BRITISH RAIL ENGINEERING LTD.

TRAINING AGREEMENT

This Agreement made the ....**Fourteenth**........ day of ....**August**........ 19**78**.......BETWEEN...**Harry Royston ROBERTS**........
Works Manager, Swindon Locomotive, Carriage and Wagon Works...........
on behalf of BRITISH RAIL ENGINEERING LTD. (hereinafter called "the Company") whose registered office is at 274/280 Bishopsgate, in the City of London, of the first part, and ....

........................**Ronald James BATEMAN**........................ of
........................**14 Lovell Close, Covingham, Swindon**........................
in the County of.........**Wiltshire**.......................(hereinafter called "the Guardian") of the second part, and ...**Ronald Neal BATEMAN**........................
.... of ..**14 Lovell Close, Covingham, Swindon**......
........................in the County of **Wiltshire**........
(hereinafter called "the Trainee") of the third part.

WHEREAS–

1. The Trainee has completed a period of probation from the ....**Fifth**........day of........**September**........19**77**.......to the ....**Twenty Fourth**........day of........**February**........19**78**.....and has attained the current statutory school leaving age or 16 years whichever is the less.

2. The Company are willing to accept the Trainee to be taught and instructed as ....**a Vehicle Painter**........................

3. The Guardian having enquired into the nature of the business conducted by the Company desires that the Trainee shall be taught and instructed as ....**a Vehicle Painter**........................ in the service of the Company.

Now it is hereby AGREED as follows:–

(1) The Trainee, of his own free will and with the consent of the Guardian, hereby binds himself as Trainee to the Company as ....**a Vehicle Painter**........................ on the conditions hereinafter appearing, and on the Company's Conditions of Service for the appropriate Adult staff, except in so far as the latter are not consistent with the conditions set out in this Agreement.

My training agreement was signed by Harry Roberts (Works Manager), my father (guardian) and myself (trainee). The agreement effectively bound me to the works for the duration of my apprenticeship.

opportunity to reaffirm the instructions he had been given prior to his arrival in Swindon, a directive to close the works down. He told of how he had liked what he saw when he had first seen for himself the Swindon workforce in action, and told us how much he admired the dedication and the spirit of the men. His enthusiasm thus compelled him to return to the Board of Directors of British Rail Engineering and explain to them that he didn't in fact want to close the Swindon Works, on the contrary, he insisted that he wanted to keep it open. We had no cause to doubt him, for never did a man sound more sincere, and the works was indeed still going strong when Harry Roberts finally retired in 1981.

More than forty years has now passed since the day I first entered the BREL Works Training School in Swindon. Prior to relocating overseas in 2016, I used to regularly get together with a few colleagues from the 1977 intake, and somehow we always finished up reminiscing about the school and about how much we enjoyed our time there.

> The Works Training School was the spawning ground for a hundred trainees, all brought together from various industries in the town. A wonderful platform for all to unconsciously grow into adulthood, and learn both technical and, unwittingly, social skills. That first year of our working lives proved to forge not only our foundation in working life, but our friendships for the rest of our lives. At the end of the year, we all went our separate ways, back to our parent companies, but those friendships continued for a lifetime.
>
> Keith Shailes, technical apprentice, 1977 intake

The same could be said by those apprentices who began their training at the school in the previous decade.

> I always remember the bright lighting, the strange machinery and the excellent manner in which the instructors taught us at the Training School – not like one or two other teachers I'd come across. I'm so glad I started my working life there.
>
> Stan Scott, Trimming Shop foreman, 1964 intake

Over the years, the instructors we remember so well have taken on a legendary status among us. Social media has ensured that reunions of ex-apprentices from all the various intake years are now commonplace. It is always good to read about the experiences of others who passed through the school during its twenty-odd operational years. None more so than the recollections of Yvonne Cross (née Bradshaw), the solitary girl apprentice among 100 boys, who successfully completed her first year of training at the school in August 1978:

> I feel privileged to have been born into a time that enabled me to attend the British Rail Training School as one of the first female engineering apprentices. I am grateful for the opportunity to have worked at British Rail, which at that time was one of the most respected industries in the world. I am also thankful to the boys in my year and the staff who got me over the finish line at the end of the year.
>
> The school was a huge learning experience for me both in manual skills and personal growth. My future husband was one of the 100 apprentices that I worked alongside at the school. The skills I learned led the way to a fulfilling and financially rewarding career in engineering and has shaped my subsequent life. Hopefully it has paved the way for future girls to have a successful and rewarding career in engineering.

These sentiments were echoed by Paul Ellis who entered the training school during its early years. His apprenticeship papers and certificates appear to have served him well throughout his entire career:

> I finished my electrical apprenticeship at BR Swindon in 1970 and went on to be an aircraft technician at Heathrow, then a computer technician and then I moved to Australia. I then discovered that licenced electricians get good money here, and so forty years after finishing my apprenticeship I dug out my papers and registered as an electrician. I'm so glad I kept all that paperwork.
>
> Paul Ellis, electrician apprentice, 1964 intake

Lesley Williams' late husband Steve was an apprentice in the 1968 intake. 'It took him into multi-disciplined engineering and design jobs; he was always very accomplished at whatever he chose to do.' Martyn Williams of the 1974 intake thought that going through the school gave everyone a good basic grounding in engineering. 'We were bloody lucky to have had the chance to do that!'

Class of 1977. The author is in the back row, eighth from the left. Jack Bevan is on the extreme left in the front row. Ron Clack is forth from the right and Tom Smith third from the right. (Roy Hazell Collection)

3

GOING INSIDE – FIRST IMPRESSIONS

Without doubt, my most memorable day during that first year at the Works Training School was the day I finally got to experience the magnificence of the Swindon Works. Having become a beneficiary of that dramatic turnaround in the works' fortunes during the mid-1970s, I was now destined to become a craftsman inside. Not only had I been offered the full four-year apprenticeship upon completion of that first year's training but I was also very likely to be offered a job thereafter as an indentured tradesmen. Once us EITB lads had agreed to join British Rail, we were effectively signing up to work within an establishment that, unlike the other BR apprentices at the school that year, we had yet to set eyes upon. Our first experience of that unknown world that lay beyond the main London to Bristol railway lines and the high red brick wall that separated the school from the works was still to come.

I confess I had no idea of the sheer enormity of the treat that lay in store for me that day. To put it into perspective, I was fortunate enough recently to have the opportunity to take a tour of the mighty Boeing assembly plant in Everett, Washington State, which at well over 100 acres is the world's largest building.[39] I remember as we commenced our tour, the guide said to us, 'Now don't go wandering off and getting lost, for it will probably take you a month to find your way out again!' This took me right back to that first tour of the Swindon Railway Works when our instructor said something very similar. On this occasion, we were about to enter the 11-acre expanse of what was once the largest building in Europe under one roof – the mighty A Shop. The sight that awaited us that day was equally as impressive as that mind-blowing aircraft assembly plant in Seattle. My first glimpse inside, followed by those first wanderings through the seemingly endless assortment of workshops that comprised the works felt like an adventure in wonderland. Even today, more than forty years later, that first sight of the A Shop resides in my memory, effectively enabling me to forever relive the experience vividly in cerebral images of yesteryear.

I remember it was an unusually hot Friday afternoon in early spring when, in the course of a safety at work seminar, we were separated into groups and taken across into the works. It was a big moment for me, as I was about to finally see the place where I was expected to complete the remaining three years of my apprenticeship. We all funnelled through the large green wooden gate set into the ageing red brick wall behind the training school, and then proceeded through the Dean Street tunnel entrance towards where the main workshops were situated. The Dean Street tunnel was one of several passages into the works. This particular access route separated the Training School from the Bristol End of the workshop system. It ran beneath all of the main Bristol to London railway lines, in addition to countless other workshop sidings. Bitumen-covered pipework ran all along the inside wall of the tunnel entrance, every so often there were small equally spaced signs saying 'No Spitting'. We had been separated into three groups of about thirty apprentices, with each group allocated to an instructor who would be our guide throughout our walk through the maze of workshops, ranging from the gigantic and overbearing to the small and intimate. We had been detailed to keep an eye open for any unsafe working practices as part of our safety at work instruction. As we walked on through the tunnel entrance the instructor who was supervising the visit kept us entertained with many stories drawn from his long experience of working inside: 'During the war years when the factory was filled with many hundreds of women, the men in charge used to bring them down into this 'ere tunnel,' he chuckled.[40] As I followed along behind, I contemplated the impact that the amplification and echoing effect of the tunnel must have had upon the kinds of noises that were presumably emanating from the tunnel entrance during those long night hours.

The Dean Street tunnel entrance was the link between the Training School and Swindon Works – the exit being opposite the mighty A Shop. (Tony Rima Collection)

When we finally emerged from the subway on the opposite side from the training school, whatever erotic thoughts this little piece of lewd history had conjured up in my mind were quickly dispelled when I captured my first memorable glimpse of the inside of the mighty A Shop. As it was a warm day, the huge double doors had been pushed twenty or so feet apart to help ventilate the vast building. As we stepped through the gap in those huge doors, those of us who had yet to experience it stood aghast with wonder at the sight that was presented to us. Immense railway carriage bodies, weighing maybe 30 or 40 tons apiece, seemed to be moving in all directions. Some were being lifted from their bogies and carried overhead by giant cranes from one set of bogies to another, while others were moving sideways along the floor on huge traversing tables. Suddenly the shout of 'Stand clear!' went up as the carriages were free-wheeled using a kind of sling and coil mechanism along internal lines from the traversing tables to the rails upon which they were to stand while being refurbished. Even the roof of this awesome building seemed to be criss-crossed with track-ways for the big traversing cranes. Written upon the great steel members that contained the crane tracks were warnings written in huge, bold lettering 'Danger – live wires'. 'Those overhead cranes, each capable of lifting 80 tons, still work as well as when they were first installed over seventy years ago,' boasted our guide as we stood aghast in admiration at another coach body being carried along sideways above our heads. I remember those huge cranes seemed to be a mixture of the latest technology, and of older cranes that had lifted some of the great steam locomotives in years gone by.

The inside of the gigantic building was so huge as to seem endless; to us lads it was as though a roof had been built on top of the world, and within a few minutes our necks had begun to ache from all the staring upwards in wonderment. The huge iron columns that supported the structure stretched far into the distance, as did dozens of pits, most of them 100 yards long and mostly thick with grease and oil built up over decades. 'They call this building "The Cathedral of Engineering",' said our instructor as he led us through the maze of railway lines embedded into the floor of the workshop. He often found himself walking alone, and had to keep stopping to wait for us as we stood there mesmerised by the collection of activities going on around us. I was not the only former apprentice to be overawed by that first experience. In *Railway Voices 'Inside' Swindon Works* (Matheson, 2008), Gordon Dickenson recounted his first experience of the works, 'This, for me, was probably the most exciting day of my whole apprenticeship. I was not disappointed. It was fantastic! The enormity of everything. The sounds, the smells of the machines, the buildings, but most of all the men.'

Dickinson's full recollections of the activities he witnessed are extensive and brilliant! 'In my instance, nothing could have prepared me for the amazing spectacle that lay beyond those towering, yet familiar red-brick walls. It was like stepping into a different world, something way beyond our imagination as though I had arrived on the set of the sci-fi epic *Metropolis*.'[41]

Another Hunslet locomotive for Kenya nearing completion. (Andy Binks, The Swindon Society)

As we moved along from one section after another, it wasn't long before it was us who had to wait for our guide, for he seemed to know everyone with whom he came into contact, and after a couple of quick conversations with various fellows that he knew, we never really got very far in the first half-hour. 'You can sometimes go years without seeing someone in 'ere,' he would say, 'Then all of a sudden they just spring out at yer, an' then you can be stood there talking for ages.' Although there were no steam locomotives to marvel at, we were suitably impressed by the line of new Hunslet shunting locomotives for Kenya Railways that many believed had given the works that new lease of life that I referred to earlier. These locomotives were all lined up parallel to one another at the far end of the A Shop, and all at different stages of assembly.

I also remember catching sight of one of the high-speed oil-rig boats under manufacture for Nigeria, and being totally confused as to why British

Rail appeared to be building boats. Only recently when I began researching what I'd written down all those years ago did I discover the answer.

As we ventured on through each different department inside the A Shop, you quickly forgot that you were still under the same roof, for, although the A Shop was classified as one big workshop, it consisted of countless other internal shops, all of which were staffed by different 'gangs' of men, each gang allied to a certain trade. Although I didn't know it then, the 'gang' was then split into various levels of an invisible hierarchy, depending on each man's level of ability and his length of service. Another thing I noticed was that a lot of the men had different coloured overalls. Apprentices were always in green boiler suits, while the skilled tradesmen had blue bib and brace overalls. The welding and fabricating trades tended to have brown overalls and often the shop number would be stencilled on the back. Our instructor said that in most cases all the men within the gang worked in pairs, and the guy that you were paired up with was forever referred to as 'your mate'. 'The worst thing you could ever do was to turn up at tea break without your mate,' he continued. In time I would discover that he was right in this respect.

Overhead view inside A Shop showing one of the more recently installed overhead cranes. (Tony Rima Collection)

During that first walk through, our guide could not help but continue to explain about the way things were always organised inside and about what we should expect when our time arrived to come over to the main workshops. 'Notice how each gang of workers has its own hut or partitioned area for break times,' he pointed out. We peered into a hut containing several chairs and a table, all neatly covered with blue factory-issue tissue paper intended to serve as a makeshift tablecloth for when tea breaks were taken. When I started in the workshops, I remember the 'tablecloth' was always renewed at the end of each week – each man on 'the gang' was expected to take his turn at performing this task. Tea urns intended to serve several gangs were situated at various sites throughout the shop, and some labourers would gladly assume the responsibility for keeping it topped up and making sure it was always boiling at the correct times.

The tea break area was always adjacent to the chargehand's box. 'That's so he can keep an eye on how long the men are spending having their tea breaks,' said our instructor. The chargehand's box was rather like a garden lock-up consisting of a high stool and small desk beneath a few shelves. Upon these shelves were books containing the numbers of hours worked by each member of the gang on a particular job, often going back years, sometimes even for decades. Most chargehands liked to have their names neatly signwritten across the top of the door, and one of the perks of being a chargehand was that you could hang your coat on the inside of the door, rather than in a bank of lockers that was probably situated more than 100 yards away. I also remember that the chargehand always read his paper and ate his lunch in the box, separate from the men, and occasionally his head would poke out to respond to comments that were made around the table.

Each area of the A Shop seemed to have its own smell that hung permanently in the air. That smell generally depended on the various oils and solvents that the work in that area incorporated, and the sides of all the gangways were festooned with toolboxes, chairs and benches of all shapes and sizes. The lockers and cupboards often had the owner's name and check number neatly signwritten on the door using elaborate lettering with shading. The prominence of signwriting seemed to be reflected on sign boards in every building throughout the works as if those particular tradespersons coveted every opportunity to display their skills. Knowing I would soon be learning this particular skill, I often lingered whenever I saw a signwriter in action, or when I noticed a man painting the yellow and black chevrons on the back of the shunting locomotives using a fine lining brush.

You had to tread very carefully as you progressed through the works as there were many things you could either trip over or fall into. Large sections of the factory floor were made up of wooden blocks that were black from years of grime, and might occasionally come lose or pop out. You also had to be wary of the abundance of inspection pits between the internal railway lines. It was noticeable that these pits tended to accumulate a fair amount of litter on account of people using them like rubbish bins. It was clearly evident that the strict emphasis that the Works Training School had placed upon health and safety was not so rigidly adhered to inside the factory workshops. After we had completed our visit, we were asked to note down any instances of unsafe working practice we had witnessed throughout our tour on a sheet of A4 paper. These were soon filled on both sides before we had even finished recollecting what we had witnessed. The wearing of safety goggles, safety shoes and ear defenders was not so rigidly enforced in the workshops, and employees seemed to be able to smoke whenever and wherever they pleased. A number of outdated and faded safety posters were evident, as were lists of factory regulations, usually on display close to one of several clocking-in racks throughout the workshop. To its credit, the works adhered very closely to current fire regulations, each area being properly assessed and fire extinguishers of all types evident in areas where they might be required. This probably had something to do with the works having its own exclusive fire station, a place where all apprentices were given appropriate firefighting instruction and also lectured on which extinguishers to use for different types of fires.

Across from the A Shop, on the other side of the Rodbourne Road Bridge, stood No. 9 Engine Repair Shop. This was a long, narrow building that consisted of two straight, uncluttered gangways running the length of it, each bisecting huge collections of stripped-down engine components all at various stages of repair or reassembly. Throughout the tour our guide had more than once stopped somebody and introduced us to him. Upon entering the engine repair shop he called one fellow over and informed us, 'Now then gents, who are the painters among you?' Me and two other lads half raised our hands and stepped forward. 'Right then you three,' he continued, 'This chap 'ere's gonna be yer Shop Steward. Any problems yer

The A Shop toilet block was mounted just under the roof of the largest workshop in Europe – to save space! (Jason McCormick/Neil Lover, Swindon's Other Railway)

No. 9 Engine Repair Shop days before closure. (E.J. Jefferies Collection)

get when yer come on over, 'ee's the bloke yer go an' see.' The huge, jolly-faced man with thick black eyebrows and a big black moustache winked at us all as he splashed another brush full of disgusting-smelling aluminium paint over a huge section of engine casing. On the next bench his pal was coating the inside of the casing with a solution of red oxide paint that stank so abominably it made your head swim.[42]

Almost all the workshops were noisy, warm and smelly, yet always seemed to maintain a cheerful atmosphere, occasionally fostering an impression of men working contentedly together as though they were children playing with toys. Men who we had never seen in our lives would wave at us, wink or smile and say hello as though they were welcoming us on board a cruise liner. For a fleeting moment I started to regret that it would be another four or five months before we would be coming over to the works permanently.

As we continued our wanderings through No. 9 Shop, I began to wonder if this engine repair shop might at one time have been the iron foundry, for, as like many of the smaller workshops, the walls were adorned with all kinds of memorabilia from the golden era of the GWR. Among the many famous old nameplates, I remember a huge plaque on the west wall celebrating the casting in 1950 of the nameplate for *The Princess Elizabeth*, 'Cast in Her Majesty's Presence'. Another plaque commemorated the royal visit of King George V and Queen Mary in 1924. Other nameplates included *The Great Bear*, the first Pacific-class locomotive built in 1908, and *The City of Bath*, one-time holder of the world speed record. Along with the old GWR fire buckets and old headlamps with bullseye lenses, these trophies from the past seemed to contrast sharply with the gleaming rows of cylinders and crankshafts that now symbolised a new railway era. Many of the workshops contained memorials to those among them who had fallen in two world wars, and I gathered that wreaths were laid or hung alongside them every Armistice Day. All these relics and emblems from a bygone era were genuinely cherished for the sake of the railway employees on the shop floor, for they existed as an everyday representation of their heritage from their fathers and grandfathers. I have no doubt that they further reinforced the feelings of pride at belonging to the Railway Works.

Incredibly, I'm also inclined to admit that another memorable aspect of my first sortie inside the railway works was my first ever encounter with pornography. It may seem unbelievable today, but at 16 years of age I had very rarely – if ever – set my young eyes upon explicit photographs such as these. The walls of many of the workshops, particularly in the areas where the men ate their lunch, were adorned with images of naked women. Additionally, a pile of well-thumbed issues could be seen stacked high on a side table. Our guide, who I later found out to be a religious man, was very uncomfortable about this sort of thing, and I remember an instance later on in the tour when in a lightning fit of temper he tore a full-frontal nude photo off of the wall before our eyes and then simply carried on talking as though it hadn't happened. For seventy or so apprentices who would be entering the workshops for the first time that summer you can imagine such a thing elicited much stifled laughter.

The spaces between the various workshops were often as busy as the workshops themselves as small yellow trucks, carrying either materials or gangs of men, consistently shuttled from one end of the works to the other. Upon approaching every entrance and exit to the workshops you had to listen for the sound of a horn, for you had to be very careful that the yellow forklift or flatbed trucks didn't suddenly push the rubber doors back into your face. There was certainly no shortage of two-wheeled traffic as men whose job required them to visit several areas throughout the vast expanse of workshops were able to use their bicycles to get around much quicker. Strictly speaking, you were only allowed to push the bicycle inside the workshops, but this rule was regularly flouted inside the massive A Shop, which was almost as long as the rest of the works itself. Upon exiting the engine repair shop, we crossed another busy thoroughfare before entering the wheel shop, where row upon row of wheel axles, some rusty and some freshly blackened, were spread over a large area. For a gang of lads who only a few weeks earlier had gained their first experience of operating a centre lathe, the sight of these huge wheels being skimmed between centres was quite something to see. We were also shown the site of the old wheel presses that, when operational, could be heard as far away as the town gardens – or so we were led to believe.

On through the wheel shop we eventually came into No. 19 Shop and an area where armies of carpenters, fitters and other vehicle-body finishers were working on a variety of diesel multiple units all mounted on huge orange-coloured jacks. It was evident from the smell that various gluing and fibreglass compounds and epoxy resins were used extensively in this area. All the carriages were positioned between wide, wooden planking duckboards for the purpose of easy access. The duckboards had to be wide to accommodate the usual collections of toolboxes, workbenches, tables and chairs, etc.

You then entered another long workshop with huge ventilators in the roof that was known as the Diesel Testing House, where it could become incredibly noisy when two or three engines were being tested at the same time. The men who worked in the pits in the testing bays would occasionally emerge from the underside of an engine covered from head to foot in grime or blackened oil. All these work bays were served by a huge traversing table outside at the rear of the building, upon which all the carriages waiting to be worked out in the yard would be loaded and then fed into the particular work area.

The final workshop at the end of the No. 19 Shop building that ran parallel to the Testing House was the Paint Shop, a place where in the not too distant future, I would be required to work for a number of years. More about the Paint Shop later, for on the other side of the gangway, running adjacent to the Paint Shop was the Paint Stores and the Polishing Shop with its own collection of smells. As you progressed through the door at the end of the gangway you were back out into the open air, staring at the entrance to the main office building.

Around the corner of the office building was the Spring Shop, a very hot and noisy working environment where it seemed to me that the use of ear defenders was an absolute must, yet I never saw a single pair being worn. In the centre of the Spring Shop, a man referred to as a 'striker' would feed the lengths of steel into a huge press for the ends to be hammered into shape before being fed into the coiling machine. Alongside was the foundry where we were afforded a fleeting glance around the door at the activities in progress in this particularly hot environment. Upon seeing molten metal being poured into a mould for the very first time, I thanked my lucky stars that I would not be required to work in what appeared to me to be a potentially dangerous place.

Prior to the long walk back to the Training School, we were afforded a quick glimpse inside the main office building. The thing I remember most about the offices, apart from the very rare yet welcome sight to all the lads of the office girls, were the countless reminders of a more glamorous past that here and there were screwed to the walls. These including the nameplates of some of the great locomotives associated with Swindon Works and the Great Western Railway. In the conference room hung the nameplate for

The North Star, built on Tyneside by Robert Stephenson, the locomotive brought into service to pull the very first passenger train in 1838 and implicit in the early success of the GWR. Also in this conference room we were shown that aforementioned device formerly owned by Isambard Kingdom Brunel and used for measuring his original 7ft-wide lines, before finally giving way to 4ft 8½in standard gauge. We were also shown how the offices had been built with twin sets of windows as a measure to guard against the noise of the steam locomotives operating at all hours. Visitors to the main offices were often invited to sit in the much-coveted chairs that were embossed with the old GWR logo.

Returning back towards the tunnel entrance, we were led through another area where a large crane with its operator sitting on board ran along the floor on tramlines, usually carrying a large gearbox or some other huge engine component that had recently been assembled. Beyond this, we passed through another large shop with lines full of wheels and bogies, before passing through an enclosed tunnel that actually served as a bridge over Rodbourne Road.

The corridors of the main office building were adorned with memories of the glory days of the GWR. (E.J. Jefferies Collection)

Emerging from the building on the other side, there was a huge canteen on the right, and on the other side of the small car park outside there was a large turntable and a couple of early diesel-hydraulic locomotives that were permanent exhibits. On the other side stood the mighty A Shop, which we re-entered through the right-hand door into the Machine Shop. There engine and body parts of all shapes and sizes were skimmed, milled, ground and turned on an army of centre lathes, grinding and milling machines. Our first-aid instructor was the foreman of this particular area, and frequently joked to us that his men had an easy time of things on Friday afternoons while their boss was away teaching the apprentices first aid. It certainly showed! To the right of the walkway was where most of the bench-fitting work was done, and beyond this machining shop was a large sheet metal/fabrication area where various internal and external body panels were formed or welded together. They also made carriage lamps for the backs of wagons in this area, and it always amused me to see the long line of car exhausts and radiators that workers had brought into the sheet metal compound to be repaired. Beyond this area was the huge traversing table and after what seemed like an eternity, we were back where we had started, standing beneath those huge yellow cranes passing overhead with their bogie-less railway carriages hanging beneath.

So I had finally been inside the Swindon Railway Works and experienced the magnificence of it with my own eyes. As a Swindon lad, born and bred, it felt to me as though I had suddenly experienced this whole new world on my own doorstep that I had previously never known existed. I was astounded that for all of my days as a young lad growing up in Swindon, this giant commune of mechanical activity had lain hidden away beyond those vast red brick walls, constructions that I had previously only ever considered as boundaries that lined the main roadways heading towards the town centre. How many other workshops, sheds and other railway buildings were yet to be discovered among this sprawling network of railway lines? Those other workshops I would certainly discover in good time, particularly when I spent a six-month period of my apprenticeship on the maintenance gang. These people, bedecked in huge white donkey jackets, would often venture into areas where few were allowed to tread. It struck me at the time that the more remote from the main entrances the workshops were, the more tightly knit were the gangs that functioned inside them.

I remember as we prepared to return back to the Training School through the Dean Street tunnel entrance, I noticed a few of the apprentices bashfully rolling their sleeves down to hide a little secret that they had been unable to contain as they toured the works, their addiction to trainspotting. I never truly imagined that such an age-old hobby as trainspotting still held its grip upon the youth of that particular era, until I saw half a dozen of the lads pulling up their sleeves and frantically writing carriage numbers on their arms. Their secret was out and the ribbing would begin in the canteen as soon as we reached the other side!

That first trip through the works was without question the most unforgettable experience of my time inside. Occasionally during reflective moments, now thirty-four years after closure, I find it very easy to close my eyes and mentally re-walk the journey from one end of the Swindon Works to the other. From the mighty A Shop at the Bristol End a few hundred yards in and out of various workshops to the office building at the London End of the works, I often believe I can still recall every smell, every face, every machine and so many other details right down to every girlie poster and every bit of graffiti along a route that I must have trodden a thousand times or more. Sadly, it has been the many journeys during the final few months of Swindon Works that recur in dreams more consistently than the time of that first memorable visit back in 1978, the days when every workshop was a hive of activity. Generations before me would undoubtedly recall their memories of working inside those workshops as a truly magical time, especially when spent inside workshops filled with steam locomotives during the glorious days of the Great Western Railway era. In contrast, I and thousands like me are much more likely to remember the ghostly atmosphere inside each of the workshops, which towards the end and Black Wednesday had become a vast collection of near-deserted buildings. To think that within ten years those bustling workshops, including the 'cathedral of engineering' that I witnessed that day, would be staffed by just a handful of hangers-on as the final closing date loomed for the doomed works.

Before any of that happened, I had a trade to learn, and barely four or five months after that first visit my time at the Works Training School would be complete. In August 1978, I was transferred over to the main Swindon Works to begin the second year of my apprenticeship inside the magnificent A Shop. The contrast between this and my first year at the Works Training School couldn't be more marked, and is worth describing in the next chapter in some detail!

4

BECOMING A PAINTER

Just one week after leaving the Works Training School I commenced the second year of my apprenticeship inside Swindon Works. That highly enjoyable year at the school would soon fade into a distant memory now that I was finally working 'in among the men'. I had a trade to learn, an additional vocabulary to learn (some of the words being more colourful than others!), and what seemed like a never-ending labyrinth of workshops to negotiate, as well as the usual initiation pranks that apprentices had endured for decades.

No. 19 Paint Shop was situated at the extreme London End of the workshop complex and was directly adjacent to the main office building, separated only by the walkway and the slope that lead to the main London Street tunnel entrance. It was a long, narrow workshop containing two sets of railway lines, approximately 5 or 6m apart, and it was usual for each line to contain up to four multiple unit coaches, all at various stages of being worked upon. Two great long steam pipes were laid alongside the rails to assist in maintaining the correct temperature conducive to the work that was being done there, be it cleaning, stripping, stopping up, polishing or painting. At the front of the shop stood the two chargehands' boxes and a long table with an assortment of seats on one side, and a long bench seat backing on to steel lockers on the side opposite. There were cupboards of all shapes and sizes situated around this area, all neatly signwritten by the gang signwriters. On the walls above were a collection of long, meticulously signwritten carriage nameplates from years gone by, bearing famous names associated with the GWR – services such as *The Bristolian*, *The Cornishman*,

The Merchant Venturer and *The Cornish Riviera*. On the other side of the gangway, at a suitable distance from the category four painter chargehands, was another box belonging to the chargehand who oversaw the work of the category one, two and three men. Next to this chargehand's box was a tall cupboard that was usually filled with pre-ordered vegetables that had recently been harvested from his allotment. These he would sell to his regular punters throughout the course of the day.

On my first morning inside the workshops I was assigned to one of the two coach painter chargehands, a short, friendly-looking old fellow, not much taller than 5ft. Upon being introduced to him by my apprenticeship module controller, he looked me up and down while keeping his hands in his pockets, then said in a tone of disinterest, 'C'mon then Ron. I'd better take you over to see Eric first,' Eric being the Paint Shop foreman.[43]

Thereafter, I had to be marched back out of the Paint Shop, across the whole of No. 19 Shop, and then up a flight of stairs on the other side of No. 20 Shop. Reflecting upon my first meeting with Eric – a short, round-faced, balding man of many chins – probably about 60 years of age, all I can say is that it was probably the only occasion during the remainder of my apprenticeship that we engaged in something approaching a civilised conversation. I quickly learned from the men that, with regard to this particular foreman, he either liked you or he disliked you – there was no in between. If he liked you, he was like a favourite uncle towards you, forever offering sweets and seeing to it that you got a more than fair crack at the better jobs. If he disliked you, you no longer existed from that moment on, unless of course you broke the rules. From that day onwards he completely ignored me, and that meant I was rooted firmly in the latter category. Later in the course of my apprenticeship I would often be the target of his fury when he would give me a dressing down for the pettiest of misdemeanours, such as working without clean overalls or being caught chatting with other apprentices. I soon learned that it was a wise move to immediately take a detour if I saw him coming towards me, or if I turned a corner and saw him coming, I quickly did an about-turn and darted back from where I came from. More often than not I was spotted, and he would bellow at me, 'What the bloody hell do you think you're doing?' And then when he caught up with me he would shout into my ear, 'If you want fun and games lad, I'll give you fun and games,' and then he would take hold of my arm and drag me off back to where I was supposed to be working and give my elders a dressing down for allowing me to wander off. All of us lads were both fascinated and terrified of him, and we used to joke that one day he would get so wound up that his huge neck would explode. I later learned that in his younger days, Eric had been a very gifted craftsman, winning all sorts of signwriting competitions, etc. Despite his questionable approach towards us painting apprentices, I've no doubt that he more than merited his high station.

Aside from meeting the section foreman, that first morning was going to be an enlightening experience in more ways than one. Not only was I to begin learning my allocated trade, there was also that new rail works vocabulary to take on board – the well-known and the not so well-known. My indoctrination began the moment I left the foreman's office. 'Come on then, Ron,' said the first chargehand who had been introduced to me as Nobby. 'Let's take a walk up the pub.' *The pub*? I looked at Nobby in amazement. It wasn't yet lunchtime, not even morning break, and here we were 'going up the pub'. My expectations soon diminished when we went outside into the yard behind the Paint Shop where rows and rows of railway carriages were lined up waiting to enter the workshops to be refurbished. 'These are the coaches waiting to come into the shop,' said my leader. 'I take a look round 'ere now and again just to see what's about – I always say to the blokes I'm just going up the pub.'

That was the way of things during that first few weeks, a new vocabulary often evolving out of practical jokes played out on the uninitiated – in other words, me! When we got back inside, Nobby took out a wad of transfers from inside his box and said to me, 'Will you take these stickers to Charlie outside on B Shed Four.' 'OK,' I said, thinking to myself that it wasn't possible that I would not be able to find a large shed outside of the main building. Upon exiting the shop, I couldn't see anything resembling a shed, except for a small, wooden hut about 200 yards away. I set off towards the hut in the direction of what I assumed to be 'B Shed Four' and, upon arriving at the small building I could see there was no Charlie to be found anywhere. I went back to the Paint Shop, where the chargehand was waiting for me outside. 'Where 'ave you been?' he enquired. 'Where's B Shed Four?' I replied. 'This is B Shed Four,' he said and pointed to a stretch of line on a siding containing two railway carriages. I'm sure that particular chargehand was secretly enjoying this indoctrination, and I remained baffled for many years over why that particular stretch of siding was always referred to as 'B Shed Four'.[44]

Looking through some of the comments by other apprentices, I doubt whether anyone coming over from the Training School escaped these petty initiations:

> The Works Training School had been very well organised as you went from section to section. We were just boys then fresh out of school. It had been a nice soft transition before the rigours of the Swindon Works proper. On my first day there I was sent to the stores for a long weight!
>
> Paul Ellis

Fifth-generation railwayman Tony Rima, who completed his apprenticeship as a coach finisher in the early 1960s, was also a victim of one of the many practical jokes played on new apprentices:

> I was not sent to get a rubber hammer of a bucket of steam. I was sent to the far side of 15 Shop (some half-a-mile or more) with a billy-can to get water from a tap there as it was colder. It took me a while to twig what was going on, but I didn't mind as my Uncle Ron worked there and my Uncle Charlie worked next door in 14 Shop (blacksmiths), and so I took the opportunity to visit them.

After tea break, I was transferred to another arm of the coach-painting department at the opposite, or Bristol End, of the works – right down at the far end of the big A Shop. Because it was allied to No. 19 Shop, the department was always referred to as 19A Shop. I was put with two fellows, both from the same outlying village, who would take me under their wing and show me the ropes. Usually when you were paired up with someone else to work alongside, he was always referred to as 'your mate', but because I was the apprentice for the next three years I would always be referred to as 'the boy'. 'Let the boy do that job,' 'Give that to the boy to do,' 'Did you make any tea for the boy' – I got it every day for five days a week. If I put my hands into my pockets it was always, 'Get yer gloves off boy!'

The thing I remember most about my first days in the workshops under the care of my two new overseers, Dennis and Doug, is that they possessed certain habits and mannerisms that I simply had never been familiar with.

I was completely taken aback by their regular use of the foulest language, habitual cussing and swearing as well us constant explicit sexual references of a type to which I had seldom been exposed. Neither had I ever been fascinated with wrestling or horse racing, nor even drinking as much beer as ones disposable income would allow. My own father was a foreman at another engineering firm, and although he smoked and occasionally swore, it was always done covertly or under his breath so that my mother couldn't hear. I suppose we had become a bit less working class, just by the fact that my dad was in charge of people and often went to work in a suit. I just wasn't used to being around grown men persistently mouthing obscenities, continually squabbling among themselves and smoking virtually non-stop. This was not something specific to that day and age either; Hugh Freebury, in his account of being an apprentice in the 1930s, experienced a similar measure of discomfort for the same reason:

> Although boys referred vaguely to the facts of life at school, I was not quite prepared for such frequent references to these things, but soon found myself having to accept it as part of the earthiness and monotony of the manual worker's daily existence, though I felt no desire to participate in such banter myself.

Another reason my two charges seemed to be persistently on edge was their level of anxiety about whether or not the weekly productivity bonus or 'balance' was going to be up or down. If it was up, the men went about their tasks with extra vigour and even displayed a hint of a smile. If it was down, the vitriol sometimes went on for days. As I understand it, the productivity bonus was phased out when the works won the Southern Region EMU contact in 1979. There wasn't much talk about the questionable long-term future of the works at that time. However, it was evident, even when I began at the works in 1978, that those employees who had been affected by the large-scale cuts of the 1960s always viewed with suspicion every item of news that appeared on the shop notice boards and every important visitor who stopped to cast a roving eye upon the current workload.

The dominant man of my two new overseers was Doug, an obese, pasty-faced man in his mid-50s, who chain-smoked and always used the foulest language at every opportunity. He made it clear to anyone prepared to listen that he always had his five or six pints of beer every evening, and I don't think I ever heard him refer to his 'missus' by her name. The quieter (and friendlier) of the two men was Dennis, who also chain-smoked and had a reputation for being incredibly lazy and tight with money – and his 'mate' was always ready to let him know it. The pair were both regular boozers at the same local hang-out, and would continually have childish squabbles over the pettiest of things. In between the times when they were not arguing, all the other gang members took turns at being the chief object of their contempt, with the hottest coals being reserved for the gang's most senior tradesman. I remember just after I had been introduced to these guys, the dominant one pointed out to me this tall, elderly looking man, and after telling me his name, went on to vilify him using the most disgusting language imaginable. For the next six months this old stager, who had already introduced himself to me and seemed to me to be a decent enough chap, was referred to in the most repellent manner. The reason for such hatred towards this man was merely the fact that he was the department signwriter, and would often drag this aspect of the job out, allegedly so as to avoid the hard-graft aspect of coach painting.

I found all this petty hatred and foul-mouthed abuse both strange and amusing, especially after the relaxed atmosphere of the Works Training School, where obscenities were strictly forbidden and everyone had always communicated with each other in a civilised fashion. I had never envisaged that grown men could act in such a manner, continually venting their hatred over such trivial matters. I even started to wonder why the Works Training School had gone to great lengths to turn out 'good citizens' if this was the environment they were being flung into – a place where in all likelihood they would fall into the same habits because that was just the way things were.

Stan Scott had started his working life in the training school way back in 1964 and still remembers the difficult transition from the School to the works proper to this day: 'A year after starting at the School, I was wrenched out of that brilliant place and plummeted into the grim reality of Swindon Works – in my case 24 Shop – now the site of today's North Star College.'

Fortunately, as my apprenticeship progressed, I discovered that my two new 'mates' turned out to be the exception rather than the rule. There was never going to be any escaping their colourful dialogue, and I very quickly got used to it. I also remember that when I arrived at work each morning (usually with only a couple of minutes to spare), most of the gang would greet me with theories as to why I looked as though I hadn't got enough sleep. I soon realised that this was just factory life and something that I just had to let go over my head if I was ever going to fit in. To make sure that I did, I generally laughed along with their jokes (even when I didn't understand them) and even threw in a few good lines of my own, even though I was only 'the boy'. 'Will you listen to the boy having a go at the men,' they would chuckle between bites of their sandwiches. I remember my mother had a habit of cutting bread too thickly so that the sandwiches I took to work were always a bit on the large side. Almost every day as I withdrew the sandwich from my lunchbox, someone would invariably pipe up, 'Got a bad hand then boy,' and everyone would laugh. It was incredible how much comedy mileage the men could get out of the same joke that was directed towards me during almost every lunch break.

On that first afternoon, one of the guys told me to pour some Rail Blue gloss paint into a paint kettle (never call it a pot he said). 'Put plenty of crackers in it boy,' he said. Crackers? I searched both of the Paint Section cupboards inside and out looking for a container with the word 'crackers' written on the side. 'What's up now,' he said. 'I'm looking for some crackers,' I replied. 'Here's some crackers,' he said and poured some white spirit into the paint and stirred it around. 'You've got to get used to putting a nice drop of crackers in it every time boy – but never get caught doing it! Now grab your brush and kettle and come with me.'

This was just the beginning, for later on in the afternoon he sent me to get the 'knotting pot'. After making enquiries I discovered that knotting was a shellac solution that was used to cut corners by covering a multitude of sins. It effectively negated the need for primer and undercoat in many cases by preventing the paint from seeping into absorbent surfaces. Yes – it soon became clear to me that the days of good, honest workmanship that we had heard so much about appeared to be dying out fast. Much of the the work for painters in No. 19A Shop at that time was deemed 'category three' or 'category four' by then, meaning a lot of the coaches only required partial refurbishment and a single coat of paint. Swindon had been awarded a sizeable proportion of the refurbishment of the diesel multiple unit (DMU) fleet back in 1970, but not all of this work was earmarked for complete refurbishment. Some of the units required barely a touch-up, let alone a quick lick over with gloss paint. This made things difficult for us apprentices, as we were required to complete 'phase tests' to demonstrate that we had achieved the required standard in certain disciplines. It was a good thing that later orders won by the works towards the end of the 1970s required a much superior standard of workmanship. Thereafter much of the pride came back into the quality of the work.

Some of the painting apprentices refused to yield to the age-old trick of thinning the paint, and made an extra effort to produce the best finish possible. Adrian Boast from the 1981 intake remembers this was something that rubbed some of the older hands up the wrong way:

Pete Hobbs applying transfers (No. 19A Shop). It was a job that could potentially leave you wide open to ridicule if they were not straight and correctly positioned! (Tony Rima Collection)

> The older hands used to moan at us because myself and another apprentice painted some EMU carriages and the finish was excellent – much more of a shine than normal. The old boys used to thin the paint with white spirit to make it easier to apply, but it killed the shine – our 'neat' paint always produced a much glossier finish.

As I got into the daily routine, it seemed to me that every morning began with a series of arguments between groups of painters over who had pinched whose trestle – a trestle being a long scaffold on wheels used to access the higher areas of the coaches being painted. There never seemed to be enough of these things to go around the gang, and the arguments would only be resolved by making deals for the sake of being able to get started on the job in hand. There were also regular arguments over whose turn it was to do 'the van' – usually an Express Parcels coach that required the painters to apply foul-smelling 'distemper paint' (as they called it) to the inside of the van in a confined space. If you stayed inside the job for long enough the stench would make you feel sick to the pit of your stomach.

If you had another inside job such as painting the coach ceiling then you and your mate had to acquire enough dust sheets to cover all of the trimming on the seats inside, another essential that was always in short supply and had to be fought over. For other internal work you had to liaise with other trades about having the windows open and the doors shut, or vice-versa. When you finally got working it was usually a pleasant atmosphere, the radio would be playing and everyone generally got along OK and cracked jokes and told funny stories as they worked. You soon got to know the men on the other trades and the way that they worked, so that you learned how best to accommodate each other and avoid getting in one another's way.

As the apprentice, I was constantly being reminded of the way things used to be done years ago or 'back in the old days'. If I turned up in paint-covered overalls I was forever being told, 'You would've been sent off the job years ago for turning up looking like that. In them days you wore a white overcoat and it had to be starched!' Or if I dropped the brush they would say, 'Old so-and-so would've sent you 'ome if you did that in his time. "Yer no good to me" ee'd say.'

Whenever the men stopped for a smoke, which seemed to be around every twenty minutes, I was forever stood hanging around while they recited long tales of characters who were long gone. Passive smoking was something

Preparing the coach body exterior prior to painting. (Tony Rima Collection)

unheard of then. Sometimes I would long for a tea break just to get away from the thick smoke. Even then, it was important to remember that the golden rule on every gang was that you never went to tea break or lunch, or came off the job at the end of the shift, without your mate. If it was discovered that you had simply gone off the job and left him there to finish up on his own, you were ostracised by the other members of the gang, as well as your mate when he eventually returned – usually wearing an expression as though he'd been abandoned between the trenches in No Man's Land!

The good thing about working in A Shop was that this huge building incorporated many other sections, and it was easy to give in to the temptation to wander off and talk to your apprentice mates on other sections. I quickly found my bearings in that vast building, although at first you had to be careful to retrace your steps and to memorise the order of each of the sections. One learned to pick out familiar landmarks in the same way you would when visiting an unfamiliar town or city. Depending on which side of the workshop you were walking through, it would have been very easy to get penned in if you tried to work out a short cut. From where I worked in the huge carriage-finishing section, which incorporated the entire area from the far wall to the first traversing table, I could see the sheet metal/fabrication area on the left and the huge No. 25 Shop loco-refurbishment section, which usually contained rows of shunting locomotives, cranes and many other types of specialised rolling stock. On the other side of the sheet metal section was the huge Machine Shop, while on the other side of No. 25 Shop was another traversing table and an area where the remainder of the Hunslet Shunters for Kenya were being worked upon. As the weeks passed, I discovered where all my apprentice mates in A Shop were working, and I also noticed that their overalls just got blacker and blacker as the weeks went by, whereas mine soon became an eye-catching collection of yellows, greys and blues.

I laboured away for those first few weeks without really learning anything beyond a few colourful new swear words and some assorted terms used to describe going to the lavatory. 'Take a run out,' they would say and, not having heard this expression before, I just assumed that it meant I could wander off for twenty minutes or so, which I usually did. Before going over to the works, I could already put a decent coat of paint on any surface so my day was really spent listening to their childish squabbles and occasionally disappearing off to chat to other apprentices while they sat down and had a smoke and discussed the wrestling. Of course, not everyone's experience of their first days inside was memorable for the wrong reasons. There were other pairings on the coach-painting side who took the job of training 'the boy' a bit more seriously, making sure you got a fair crack at the more challenging aspects of the job, especially the fine lining required on some of the powered coaches that made up the DMUs. Paul Armstrong has fond memories of his time on the coach-painting gangs: 'When I first went inside I remember guys shouting "No more green-backs!" Aside from that, I really enjoyed my time learning carriage-painting in 19 Shop. They were a good bunch of blokes who taught me a lot.'

Being the apprentice (or the boy) I often got lumbered with a lot of the petty little side jobs such as painting odd panels and other smaller coach parts. These were always set aside for 'the boy' – this became the case on most sections for every tedious little job that none of the men wanted to do. 'Keep those there for the boy,' was the usual directive, and I would be stood there for hours, usually painting both sides of a vast heap of radiator coverings or some other repetitive, menial task. After I had been on this department for around six weeks, I was busy painting these things when I finally had my second brush with Eric, the aforementioned Paint Shop foreman. 'Do you know what you're doing there lad?' he asked. For some juvenile reason I muttered, 'I think so.' He must have deduced from this that I hadn't the first clue what I was doing, for he marched over towards me and grabbed hold of one of these covers and said, 'Look here, you put this on the bench and give it X number of coats. Then you turn it over and give it X number of coats, have you got that?' 'Yes,' I replied. He then marched over to the chargehand and gave him an almighty rocket for not looking after the apprentice properly. Suddenly I had another enemy in the shape of the chargehand, who had been reprimanded on account of the impression I had given to the foreman of just having been left to my own devices. Not that this bothered me at the time, for I was too busy trying to work out in my mind how many coats of paint was required to give it 'X number'. Did he mean ten as in Roman numerals?

The foremen tended to spend the first hour or so of each day in their own offices, so you could usually ease yourself into the day, before having to be on your guard. Every Monday morning I had to walk the whole length of the works to change my overalls for a clean pair (I say clean, but if you were a painter, the clean overalls would still be plastered in weeks of built-up paint stains). Thinking about this weekly chore reminds me of a very strange experience I had early on in my time inside that I was never able to explain. I'll begin by stating that I don't believe in ghosts, even though I'd heard plenty of stories about the works being haunted, even to the extent that men had demanded to come off night shift after witnessing strange things. One Monday morning when I was on my way to get my clean overalls, I was walking through the tunnel that crossed over Rodbourne Road. As I emerged from the end of the tunnel and up a slope that led into an area where wheels were being stored, I noticed a figure walking towards me in starched white overalls who appeared to be staring in a strangely fixated manner straight ahead. He was walking in the dead centre of the thoroughfare and as I passed him, instead of moving to the side, he brushed heavily against me and I felt something like a chilling pain run down my arm. I gripped my elbow and spun around to look at him and he was gone – completely vanished. Even if he'd broken into a run, I would surely have seen him. For the next few years, every time I passed by that spot, I would stop and contemplate the scene and try to work out what had happened –

how did this guy just simply disappear? There was a door in the wall to the right that I never saw open, but even if he'd gone through it, I'm certain I would have heard the door. I must have shrugged the incident off after a few years when I went on nights myself, and often found myself having to walk through empty workshops that I might have once thought twice about. I always hoped I'd eventually see the man in the white overalls again and the mystery might finally be solved – but I never did.

I was not the only one to have a ghostly experience in the works, or even at that particular spot. Colin Twine conceded that he 'always walked quicker through that tunnel – it felt strange'. He also remembered a night watchman and his dog were both spooked by something in the main office building, and he refused to work nights again.

Stephanie Kaye had a strange experience while working in the outlet village on the site of the old rail works: 'Our store was in one of the sheds out the back. I'm pretty sure that when I was doing stock-check there was something in with me, washers and other small objects kept falling on the floor and I once saw a dark shadow.'

A ghostly experience occurred just before the tunnel over Rodbourne Road. (Jason McCormick/Neil Lover, Swindon's Other Railway)

Des Cook remembered that in the sidings at the bottom of Redcliffe Street there was a damaged diesel loco and it was said to have killed the driver in the accident. The vicar was called in to exorcise the cab, which Des used to run past very fast.

Since the works closed, other workers in the outlet village that replaced it have also described unusual experiences. One lady claimed to have seen a man walk straight through a wall, while another customer reported seeing a strange-looking elderly man in dirty overalls chewing tobacco in the toilets beneath the Pattern Store Bar.[45]

Whenever Thursday came around, we were required to finish a bit early at lunchtime in order to collect our pay. The payroll procedure was like a well-drilled operation, and was executed to perfection for as long as I worked inside. The men would gather on the traversing table, where two black pay tables were each erected in time-honoured fashion from three sections with almost military precision, prior to the arrival of the pay clerks. The clerks always arrived in a small, bright yellow, secured, motorised van containing the black metal pay boxes, these vans probably being the only addition to the procedure inside the past century. Inside these black boxes, all the wage packets had been arranged in numerical order for the purpose of ensuring a smooth and efficient operation. In theory, you had to queue for your wages in the correct order of your clock number, so each week you had to memorise the appearance of the person whom you followed so that you didn't miss your turn. If you did miss your turn, you had to walk the long distance to the pay office the following day to collect your pay – there was no hanging around afterwards by the payroll clerks to pay out any stragglers. As apprentices, we quickly learned that 'missing your turn' was actually quite a good 'skive', and we began to deliberately miss our turn so we could congregate and take a leisurely walk to the pay office that afternoon, or on the next day and waste a good half an hour in the process. As far as that first pay day was concerned, for an apprentice in his first week there was nothing to draw as you were always paid one week in arrears. You were merely required to go through the motions and hand in your clock card at the black table in a process that was always known as 'the grand march past'.

Things did eventually get a bit more interesting as those first weeks rolled by. As a painting apprentice I was at last afforded an opportunity to display my potential as a signwriter. Typically, the first task an apprentice signwriter was charged with would be painting the warning notices just above the tops of the bogies, the surface of which was always likely to be rough and pitted. As you went about your task of attempting to form the words 'Emergency Lighting Point' or 'Flame Switch' on these uneven, corroded surfaces, the chargehand would covertly wander along behind you assessing your ability, trying to decide whether or not you could be risked on anything more visual that would require a superior standard of workmanship. The other men on your gang would creep up behind you till they were right up against your ear and say 'got a steady hand boy', or if you were getting on well, 'Hey look, 'ee's got the touch of a midwife.'

After a week or two of trying to signwrite on these rough surfaces, the chargehand would decide whether or not you were up to the job. Apparently I made the grade and was thereafter presented with my own signwriting kit. I say 'presented' because being a signwriter was considered to be a privileged position, something to be coveted – it was like being an England cricketer and receiving your first cap! As I worked my way around the various paint shops throughout the works, it soon became clear that every gang had its own signwriter who was always proud to display his position, some even kept a pair of special 'writing shoes' so as to let the gang know he was 'going writing today' without actually saying it.

The standard 'writing kit' that you were issued with typically consisted of an assortment of writing pencils, which were actually small, black, sable hair brushes of various sizes. You were also given a lining pencil, which was a brush with a small handle containing a set of bristles about 3in long, along with a wooden palette which was about a foot square with rounded edges and a hole correctly positioned so as to accommodate your thumb. To complete the kit I was given a set of 'dippers' – small pots with hinges welded to the base allowing them to be attached to your palette, and a 'mole stick' – a 2ft length of ¾in dowel that was tapered towards one end, upon which was attached a ball of padding usually bound to the stick with a piece of leather. (This was used to steady your writing hand upon while working.) You would also be required to use a chalk line, a longish piece of string that was wound around a reel that was enclosed within an outer casing filled with powdered chalk. This would be used to 'twang' straight lines at the top and bottom of your writing surface to enable you to produce straight, uniform lettering.

GWR signwriters at work in starched white aprons. (Andy Binks, The Swindon Society)

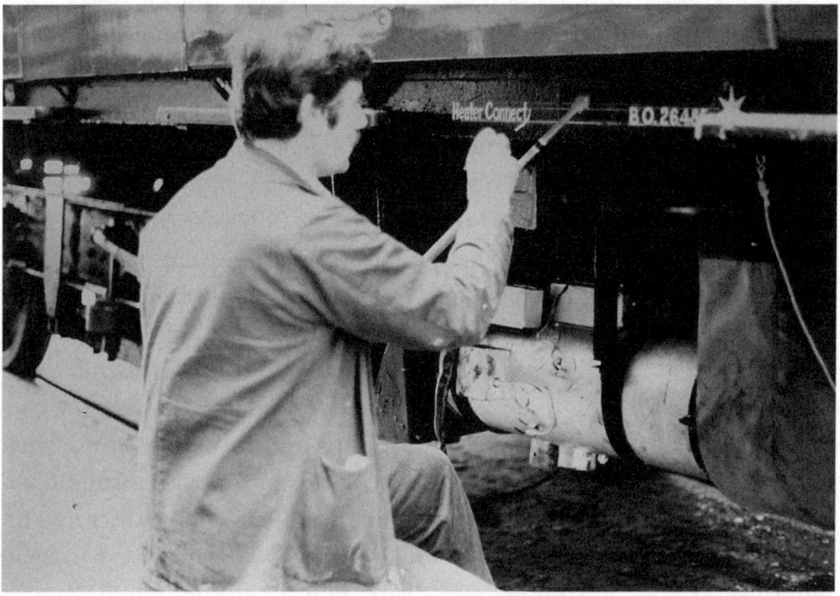

Noel Prentice signwriting warning notices on the rough and pitted surfaces beneath the carriage body. (Tony Rima Collection)

For the more important jobs you would require something called a pounce, which was simply a cloth pouch filled with chalk powder. This pounce would be tapped against a metal or cardboard stencil so that a cloud of chalk dust would be released, enabling it to leave an impression through the holes in a stencil. Finally you were given a writing stool – a small rectangular stool with a holding slot in the middle to allow it to be carried easily in and among the coaches. (The height of the stool was just about sufficient for painting the warning notices on the sides of the bogies.)

As the No. 19 Shop signwriter you forever seemed to be racing against the clock. The coaches that had to be written upon were either in the paint shop, the diesel testing bays if it was a motorised coach, or on the coach body finishing section. You could bet your last half penny that when you came in the next morning many of the coaches had been replaced by new ones, meaning those that you hadn't had enough time to complete the previous day would be halfway up the yard. This wouldn't be so bad in the summer, but on a bitterly cold winter's day it was an awful job trying to sign-write when you could hardly move your frozen fingers. So to avoid such a scenario you had to work quickly; other workers soon got used to the sight of the signwriter zipping about, darting in and out of the coaches with his palette on his thumb, gripping his mole stick in his other four fingers while carrying his stool in the other hand. There were some very gifted signwriters in the rail works during my time inside. Some of them would earn an extra few quid by giving lessons, which I used to attend in an effort to improve my skills. Eventually, I came to regard signwriting as something you couldn't really teach – you either had it or you didn't. I'm not sure I ever really had 'it'. My lettering was neat enough, though I could never have made a living at it 'outside' simply because I was never quick enough.

During the next stage of my apprenticeship I spent around six months acquiring further experience as a painter in No. 25 Shop. This was where shunting locomotives and specialist rolling stock, such as cranes, were refurbished or repaired. When I think back to my time spent working there, I seem to remember that everything we had to paint was covered in all manner of grease, oil and grime imaginable. Sometimes you would spend hours just cleaning and preparing the surfaces to be painted. 'Don't worry too much about trying to clean it all off,' the men used to say. 'Sometimes you just have to flood the paint on and seal it all up.'

They were a very nice crowd on the engine painting gang in No. 25 Shop. The work was much more varied (some of it requiring a higher skill level than I have made it sound) and the men were all very helpful. Unlike the other gangs I had been with, they all seemed to enjoy each other's company outside of work, playing in inter-shop putting competitions, etc. The whole atmosphere within their communal area epitomised the camaraderie aspect that so many former railwaymen I spoke to seem to remember. Everything, it seemed, was done 'for the good of the gang'. I remember this department had been one of the beneficiaries of that special contract awarded to the works to build the twenty Hunslet shunting locomotives for use on Kenya Railways. Bob Skinner was among the apprentices fortunate to have the opportunity to work on the one Hunslet that was to be painted in full Kenya Railways livery:

> Every day was always different as an apprentice when we finally went over to the works. I remember working on the Hunslet Shunters for Kenya – it really was a more upmarket type of job – very particular. For some reason the work was done on overtime after everyone had gone, and you had to make sure your work was perfect, as the inspection on this job was very picky.

By the time I did my stint in No. 25 Shop, the Kenya contract had almost been completed, except for a consignment of spare parts that had to be finish coated and dispatched. I can remember carefully stencilling the address for their point of delivery in Mombasa, Kenya, in black paint upon large wooden containers – all the time wishing I could travel with them all the way to Kenya.

Also while on this section, I got the opportunity to learn how to use that lining pencil that had been issued to me with my signwriting kit. The shunting locomotives were required to have neat black chevrons painted onto the yellow radiator housing, and also on the back of the cabin. Former painting apprentice Adrian Boast also liked this job, and also remembered being given a very special job while on this section:

> One of my favourite jobs was putting the wasp stripes (chevrons) on the shunting locomotives. We used to measure out the width and the position and then use chalk-lines as a guide. I also remember painting the nameplate for a loco called *Aldiniti* – after the famous Grand National

winning racehorse. The winning jockey Bob Champion was invited to unveil it, meaning it was on TV and in all the papers.

Alternatively, there were other days when the work on this department could plumb new levels of tediousness – many of the individual parts for the various items of rolling stock had to be dipped in green primer paint, prior to painting, and you just stood their dipping brackets, etc., into a basin of awful-smelling, dull green paint and hanging them above a dripping trough. At the end of the shift you finished up with this elaborate network of dripping components all somehow knitted together with hanging hooks. The next day you had to dip the same components in undercoat and then gloss on the next day. Later, during a time when the engine work dropped off, many months were spent painting 'spoil wagons' – great, long flatbed wagons that were bright yellow on the top half and dark grey on the lower half. Unlike in the carriage shop where the labourers would apply the thick black paint to the bogies and the underside of the unit, on this particular job we had to do them ourselves, and what a messy job it was.

Occasionally, while on this department you were selected for a day's work down at the Spring Shop, where all the suspension springs for the carriages were dipped into a special rubber paint solution. The dipping area was in a small anteroom, just inside the main door of the Spring Shop. It was fascinating to stand and watch the springs being made. I especially liked watching the 'striker', a big, powerful man who would stand there all day feeding each end of the red-hot material under a hammer to flatten down the ends before passing them on to his mate to heat up again and insert into the spring coiling machine.

A few years later when the works was under threat, when painting apprentices came out of their time they were being offered redeployment as a striker in the Spring Shop. It was a hard, tedious and dangerous job in a noisy environment, often working in insufferable heat. Every apprentice who I can remember being offered the job refused to take it.

When they had been sufficiently cooled, the huge springs would arrive in deep trolleys to be submerged into the respective coloured paint according to their size. They were generally far too heavy to lift, let alone lift all day long, so there was a small hand-operated electric crane for lifting the springs into the troughs full of paint and then out again. Once they were dipped, they were then placed on a special rack that would allow the excess paint to drain off and run back into the paint trough. Also in this area was a facility for spray painting the white carriage lamps. Almost every day, a huge caged trolley full of about 100 lamps would arrive. The glass would have to be masked and the lamp placed upon a revolving turntable. A sufficient amount of manual dexterity was required for this job, for the sprayer would have to operate the turntable by hand while spraying the lamp in a series of up and down movements. There was an extractor fan above the spray chamber, which I don't think was very efficient because after a long day of spraying those lamps the hairs up my nose were nearly always coated with white gloss paint. I think if I had spent too long upon this task, I would by now have become a prime candidate for a premature death from emphysema. Another problem was that the glass screen would very soon become coated with paint and this would have to be periodically cleaned off using paint stripper, the fumes of which also got right down into your lungs.

Before being assigned to whichever painting gang required my services, there was another six-month period of my apprenticeship to negotiate that was often fraught with danger. No. 34 Shop, where the workshop maintenance guys were based, was situated just behind the building that contained the starting hooter. I can clearly remember that I didn't particularly want to be in the vicinity of the hooter when it sounded – first ten minutes, and then another shorter burst five minutes prior to starting time – and then again at the designated start time itself. Because the hooter was steam-powered, every time it sounded the air all around you would be transformed into a fine drizzle of water vapour as the hooter gave a long, final decisive burst. The hooter was always sounded accurately to the second, so there was never any chance of a reprieve from this mild drenching. Men who were shuffling through the Swindon streets on their way to the works would suddenly quicken their pace upon hearing the familiar hollow, moaning noise that proceeded to a slightly higher-pitched blast. There is also a considerable history attached to this hooter. I recently learned that it sounded ten blasts to herald the beginning of the First World War and was sounded many hundreds of times to warn the town of approaching enemy aircraft during the Second World War. This was very effective, as the distinctive sound of the hooter could be heard all over Swindon and as far away as Wootton Bassett. It became an accepted feature of town life that was so familiar as to be ignored, unless you wanted to check that your watch was set at the correct time. As I said, it was a deafening, as well as a saturating experience if you happened to be right next to the thing. I was always careful to time my arrival at No. 34 Shop just right so as to avoid a drenching from the hooter.

Aside from this particular hazard, a six-month stint with the maintenance department afforded one the opportunity of working in some of the less familiar areas of the railway works complex. I had never fully realised the sheer vastness of the establishment prior to my time with the No. 34 Shop gang. Aside from painting walls and window frames, I was also required to learn the art of glazing and spent many days upon the highest roofs of the workshops replacing broken windows. As I previously indicated, this was a very dangerous time for an apprentice, especially one not used to working upon or carrying very long ladders, and quite often you were replacing panes of glass at heights of 60 or 70ft high. Another painting apprentice, Bob Skinner, almost paid the ultimate price:

> I remember during my stint with the maintenance guys in 34 Shop that you had to be a bit careful when working on top of the A Shop with its incredibly high roof. I nearly fell through while putting in some glass! If it wasn't for the blokes on the maintenance gang I would have been a goner!

I felt at the time as though I was learning a very useful part of the trade – receiving instruction on how to apply a putty bed for the glass that had to be cut to size and secured with glazing pins. The final layer of putty around the edge, nicely finished off in the angles, made for a satisfying feeling of having done a good job. Little did we know then that the growing popularity of UPVC windows would make this particular skill more or less obsolete in the very near future. I remember the men on this department set a lot of store by how well they could cut the glass to the correct size. If a piece shattered when being cut, the cutter would swear blind either that the glass was 'harder' in a particular area of the sheet or that it was too cold inside the glass store, thus causing it to break more easily.

The longer I spent in the maintenance department, the more familiar I became with the further extremes of the Swindon Works. There were so many areas of the works that I never knew existed, many of them staffed by seemingly forgotten men, all tucked away in comfortable little workshops or offices. We all used to joke that so many men appeared to do nothing all day except clock on or off – but I knew that wasn't strictly true. Also while on maintenance you were issued with a useful selection of new tools, including hammers, hacking knives, putty knives, etc. Another item of standard issue equipment was a huge, white donkey jacket, which you most certainly needed during those winter months when much of the work was still to be done outdoors.

Most mornings would begin in the same way. We would leave the department headquarters looking like an army of Abominable Snowmen, all snug inside our huge white coats. In the pockets of these coats were our tea-making things, and we would make our way to the job area, which would quite often involve climbing a long ladder to access the top of a roof somewhere. Upon arrival, the lead man would pull a teapot from his bag and say to me, 'Make the tea then boy,' then off I would go back down the ladder in search of a tea urn for hot water. Climbing back up with a pot of scalding tea was not much fun either! Much of the inside work on the maintenance gang usually involved applying a fresh coat of paint to the workshop walls or the wooden window frames. Whenever the work for the gang dried up, there was always another wall to paint somewhere in that vast expanse of workshops. All the workshop walls were painted with a pale yellowish colour called Jonquil, while all the external window frames were painted with an intense green colour called Verona. When it came to painting the walls of the mighty A Shop, the ladders would be set to such ridiculous heights that I point-blank refused to climb. I was usually detailed to stand on the bottom rung of the ladder to keep it from toppling over.

One final aspect about being in the maintenance department was that the work being done somehow made your job feel much more secure. When there was so much talk about whether or not the works had a long-term future, I often thought to myself, 'Why would we be giving these walls a fresh coat of paint or this broken window a new sheet of glass if they were simply going to close us down?'

During the later stages of my training period, apprentices were afforded a good opportunity to learn additional skills, thanks to an initiative called the Camp Coach Project. The camp coaches were old railway carriages that were to be fitted out as holiday homes for the disabled, all intended to be located at Dawlish in Devon. Works Manager Harry Roberts had been heavily involved at the design stage, having visited the Centre for the Disabled in Wales and asked to be pushed around in a wheelchair, enabling him to discover some of the physical limitations at first hand. The coaches were to be painted in classic GWR chocolate and cream livery, with the interior coachwork being polished and finished off to a very high standard. It was the first time as an apprentice that I finally got the opportunity to learn key skills such as staining, French-polishing and varnishing on large surface areas. There had been very little polishing work done at Swindon Works in recent years, meaning that all the craftsman polishers had been absorbed into the various painting gangs throughout the works. This gave rise to much shop floor banter among the men. The painters would refer to the polishers as 'rag painters', while the polishers would big their position up by referring to themselves as 'beautifiers of wood'.

This being the 1970s, the decade of lightning walkouts, flying pickets and what have you, it was soon made clear to us that another thing we would have to come to a decision about was trade union membership. British Rail Engineering Ltd, we were told, was a closed shop, meaning that, even though we were still apprentices, if we wanted to go on working as painters or signwriters, we would be required to join one of the unions. This would mean undertaking to submit a sub of something like £2 a week. All of this was contrary to my upbringing, especially in the knowledge that at the factory where my father worked, the company in question had fought tooth and nail to keep the unions out. The two main unions in BREL were the National Union of Railwaymen (NUR) and the Transport and General Workers Union (TGWU), commonly known to its members as the 'Tom and Jerry'. As a new apprentice, you tried to hold out as long as you could without signing up and paying into it until someone 'had you in a corner'. I managed to last out for about six months before the membership forms were forced into my hand. I later discovered that some apprentices who had entered the works at the same time as myself managed to avoid being rounded up by the 'union police' altogether, and had continued to work inside the rail works for more than nine years without ever having been collared by a rep. This might come across as ignorance on our part as apprentices, as though we blindly disregarded all that the unions had achieved for us before our time. Put simply, the fact that we were basically young man scraping by on 'apprentice money' meant that we were not so keen to part with our Friday night beer money for something we did not care that much about. In 1978, these unions appeared to us to represent trouble in the form of excessive militancy, disruption and an affront to personal freedom or freedom of choice. With these two powerful unions bearing down upon them, along with the train drivers' union ASLEF – which was particularly active in the late 1970s and early '80s through repeatedly calling the train drivers out on strike – the British Railways Board had a seemingly impossible task. With so much disruption, coupled with the deliberate lack of investment on the part of the government, how could they ever succeed in blowing life into an industry that was slowly bleeding to death?

Occasionally the absurdities of the days of powerful unions would be played out before our eyes when there would be meetings of all union members to ask for a show of hands over some pressing issue. These meetings were always held on the traversing table and were often chaotic and poorly organised without anyone knowing what the hell was going on. You could never hear anything, nobody ever thought to employ the use of a megaphone, and I often walked away not knowing what I had just voted for. There would often be a few militants wandering around behind everyone shouting 'one out, all out' regardless of whatever the issue was that had brought about the meeting in the first place. Of course, not long after my apprenticeship these meetings would become much more frequent when the threat of large-scale redundancies reared its head. Even then, things were so chaotic it was always advisable to buy the local paper just to get a fuller understanding about what was being communicated.

All of that was yet to come. For now, finally on the occasion of my twentieth birthday, I came 'out of my time'. This meant that my apprenticeship was completed and I was now 'one of the men'. I remember being called across to the main office building to be handed my indentures, a thick maroon-coloured wallet containing a small book in which was listed my practical and academic achievements. These included the skills that I had become proficient in, and the technical qualifications I had gained in the course of my 'not so diligent' studies at the college. I was also handed a letter that gave notice that my apprenticeship was now complete, and that my employment with British Rail had now been terminated. 'Ignore that,' said the man behind the desk, 'It's just a standard letter that every apprentice gets when he finishes his time. Consider yourself re-employed.' With that, he handed me another letter that informed me that they were now happy to reinstate me as a coach painter, my remuneration being in the region of £70 a week. I was requested to report to No. 10 Personnel Office, where arrangements would be made for my immediate reinstatement.

I arrived back on the section, where one or two of the men congratulated me: 'So you made it then, boy? Oh, hang on, we can't call you "the boy" any more.' After I'd been back on the job for about ten minutes, the chargehand came up behind me. 'You do realise Ron you will have to toe the line now that you're on the books.'

Much of my remaining five years in the works would be spent on the coach-painting sections, mainly owing to it having won the contract for refurbishing the south-coast CEP electrical unit commuter fleet in 1979. This order comprised 100 four-coach units and was a major boost for the works. From a personal point of view, it had bought me enough time to not only finish my apprenticeship, but get a good few years inside 'on the books' so to speak. Unfortunately, in an effort to keep all of the men on the painting section gainfully occupied for the remaining years, it fell upon the 'skilled' painters to clean the plastic panels and ceilings of the newly refurbished units. No proud time-served coach painter could ever put into words how much he hated and despised having to clean up the mess made by the other trades. However, this kind of thing became the order of the day; gangs were expected to take on additional tasks outside their traditional duties if they wanted to remain employed. Every item of work awarded to the gang was vital, particularly whenever rumours began that trouble in the form of job cuts could be around the corner. If any gang undertook work that had since been allocated to another department, it would invariably result in a major falling-out between management and the various unions, as well as triggering bad feeling between the departments involved.

For now I had swapped my green 'apprentice overalls' for a new set of bib and brace blue overalls – this was the mark of a category-four tradesman. The burning question I now asked myself was, 'How long would my days as a skilled craftsman at Swindon Works last?' The best answer I can give was that just over a year after coming out of my time I was given a good idea when the first major redundancies were announced in April 1982. For me, the next five years of my working life would be dominated by the slow demise and ultimate death of the Swindon Works. It is easy to forget that there was once a time when I was a craftsman inside earning a living, rather than an employee 'under threat' and staring into the abyss. When the works finally closed, I would never again earn my living with a paintbrush. Such an admission effectively renders my apprenticeship to have been largely a waste of time, yet there were other painting apprentices of my era, such as Paul Armstrong, who did make a success of it when they went 'outside' – even vehicle painting!

After the closure, I went painting and decorating for a year, before getting a job as a coach-painter for Thamesdown Transport (which has since been taken over). My apprenticeship has been invaluable throughout my career. I have painted many large vehicles over the last thirty-odd years including London Routemaster buses to preserved vintage trams and buses. I've even done a little signwriting over the years too. I have always believed we had the best training we could have had, and it always helped me with problem solving when unexpected hurdles appeared.

The Southern EMUs refurbishment contract (1979) was the last major order won by the works. This completed four-car unit is almost ready for delivery. (Tony Rima Collection)

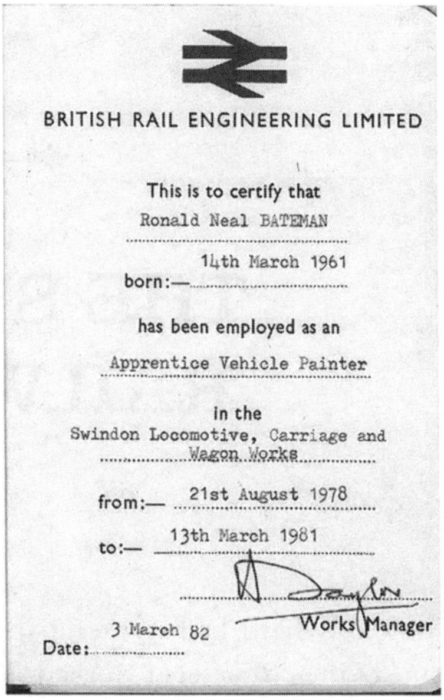

BRITISH RAIL ENGINEERING LIMITED

This is to certify that
Ronald Neal BATEMAN
born:— 14th March 1961
has been employed as an
Apprentice Vehicle Painter
in the
Swindon Locomotive, Carriage and Wagon Works
from:— 21st August 1978
to:— 13th March 1981

Works Manager

Date: 3 March 82

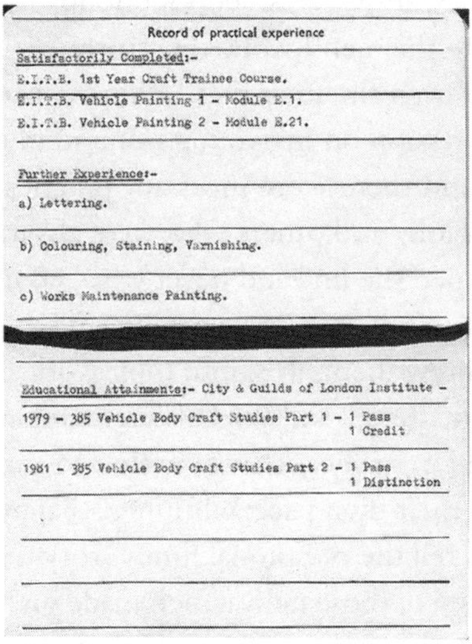

Record of practical experience

Satisfactorily Completed:-
E.I.T.B. 1st Year Craft Trainee Course.
E.I.T.B. Vehicle Painting 1 - Module E.1.
E.I.T.B. Vehicle Painting 2 - Module E.21.

Further Experience:-
a) Lettering.
b) Colouring, Staining, Varnishing.
c) Works Maintenance Painting.

Educational Attainments:- City & Guilds of London Institute -
1979 - 385 Vehicle Body Craft Studies Part 1 - 1 Pass, 1 Credit
1981 - 385 Vehicle Body Craft Studies Part 2 - 1 Pass, 1 Distinction

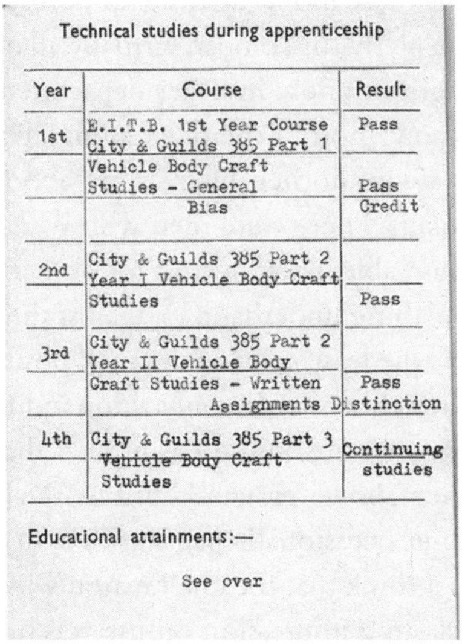

Technical studies during apprenticeship

Year	Course	Result
1st	E.I.T.B. 1st Year Course	Pass
	City & Guilds 385 Part 1 Vehicle Body Craft Studies - General Bias	Pass Credit
2nd	City & Guilds 385 Part 2 Year I Vehicle Body Craft Studies	Pass
3rd	City & Guilds 385 Part 2 Year II Vehicle Body Craft Studies - Written Assignments	Pass Distinction
4th	City & Guilds 385 Part 3 ~~Vehicle Body Craft~~ Studies	Continuing studies

Educational attainments:—

See over

Every apprentice 'coming out of their time' received a small maroon-coloured record of apprenticeship booklet outlining all of their achievements and examination successes over the course of the required training.

5

THE SWINDON RAILWAYMEN

Much of what I had written back in the early 1990s tended to focus on some of the characters I worked alongside in the railway works – the things they did and the things they said. So much everyday banter seemed to have stuck in my mind and even today, whenever I ask myself what I remember the most about my time inside, my answer will always be without doubt 'the men'. By this, I mean virtually all of them – the men I worked with, the men I got to know in other departments, and even the men that I didn't get to know: most of them left an indelible impression on my young mind in one way or another. There were eccentrics and there were incessant practical jokers. There were men who were always jolly and others who were always miserable. There were a lot of men who toed the line and never engaged in anything underhand or against the rules and others who were a bit shifty to say the least. A lot of the men positively threw themselves into their work as though it was the only thing in life that mattered, and yet I also remember men who would do as little as they could possibly get away with. Most of them, however, would just work along at their own pace; whistling a happy tune, occasionally pausing to light up and tell the occasional funny story.

I think that the chief reason why so many of those railwaymen made such a lasting impression on me was because very often your gang became like a second family. Each gang had its private hut, or its cordoned off rest area, and at either side of the shift, and also at break times and lunchtimes, the gang would typically be huddled together in intimate proximity. If you were

Vehicle builders, No. 19A Shop. That famous works camaraderie is on display in the gang communal break time area. (Tony Rima Collection)

a 'newbie' you were often excluded to the outer fringes of the group until a space became available inside the gang hut. Thereafter you had a space on the table or bench for your sandwich box, your newspaper and your mug of tea, and more importantly, you were at the very nucleus of whatever inside rivalries and petty disagreements were going on within the gang. You also picked up on all the latest gossip, and if you were a young lad you would occasionally throw in your ten cents worth, sometimes in a deliberate effort to gain further acceptance.

Nowadays workplace break times seem to pass in unbroken silence as the workforce sips its coffee and stares into its electronic devices. There were no smartphones back then, so once the paper had been read people just had to talk and have conversations – often about their home life and families, or sometimes discussing newspaper stories and current affairs. In no time at all you knew almost as much about your colleagues as you did about your own relatives. I've since worked alongside people for far longer and not known a fraction as much about their lives as I did about the men in the railway workshops. Lorne McCalla worked in No. 6 Shop and similarly missed 'the characters' more than anything else: 'Despite the grime of the place, the smell of diesel and the health issues, I missed the people – the characters were fantastic, and it was Swindon's heritage!'

Another amusing component of the inside culture of the works was that hardly anyone was referred to by their proper name. Almost everybody had to have a nickname or sorts, and you never really found out what their real name was until you saw them holding their pay card. Adrian Boast could never forget two of the nicknames on the coach-painting section:

> A standing joke with most of the apprentices in my year was the names of two blokes who were required to work together. One was known as 'Big Dick' because he was a very large man called Richard, and the other known as 'Little Willy' – because he was short and his name was Williams. We still get mileage out of that one now!

At Swindon Works, you very soon realised that not every man who went inside was there just because he needed a job. On almost every gang or department I worked on I could always spot the true railway fanatic – every gang had one, and they knew virtually everything about the railway network. These men were usually veterans of the GWR era. It was noticeable that the older Great Western men in particular took a certain pride in knowing everything about Swindon Works, past and present, and when working among apprentices they clearly enjoyed being afforded the opportunity to display their seemingly inexhaustible knowledge of each workshop's history. Working inside was merely an extension of their passion for railways – they couldn't possibly work anywhere else. They knew all the railway societies and always knew whenever the steam weekends were being held. Colleagues often used to joke that these men had steam running through their veins. The number of free passes granted to employees by BREL would never be enough for these men, so it was a good thing they had a privilege card that would entitle them to a reduced fare on the network. Every Sunday, off they would go just to be somewhere on the railway network on the days that they could not go inside. The conversation on the following Monday morning always went something like:

> 'Where did you go yesterday then Dave?'
> 'Carlisle.'

'That's a bloody long way. Any good?'

'Yeah, just had a bit of a walk around and then came back.'

Popular travel writer Bill Bryson loosely remarked that 'as long as there are steam trains in the world there are 18,500 men in Britain that will never need Viagra'. Bill was alluding to the fact that there are 108 privately run steam railways in Britain, staffed by that number of volunteers.[46] It came as no surprise to me when, after the closure of the works, I discovered a good number of these men had joined the volunteer army to do their bit towards keeping the steam locomotive alive – and I admire them for doing it.

As I moved around from department to department, or from gang to gang, the men always joked during lunchtime banter about what we might call the tightness of certain colleagues, or put another way, the typical reluctance of the older hands or more mature 'railwaymen' towards spending any money. Very early on during my time inside, I had formed the impression that a shop floor railwayman's pay was never quite enough, regardless of whatever his pay grade might have been. A lot of the men I knew had a casual little evening job 'outside', either pulling pints behind the bar or collecting up the glasses in a local working man's club – Swindon was full of them. To my mind, the typical railwayman was forever on the lookout for a means of making that wage packet stretch just that little bit further, and would rarely think twice about taking an opportunity to either save a few bob or to earn an extra buck or two when an opportunity arose. Within a day or two of going inside I was told more than once that I could use my four free railway passes to go over to Rosslare in Ireland and buy duty-free whisky and cheap cigarettes. It really was a commonly held belief or joke on almost every section I worked on that there were certain men who rarely actually bought anything; by that I mean they never spent any money if they could help it. This, of course, is a slight exaggeration, but if your young ears believed everything they heard, then this certainly seemed to be the case, particularly with the dyed-in-the-wool railwaymen – the ones who had been inside for donkey's years, and had never worked anywhere else.

When I re-read these observations I had written down so long ago, my first thought was that it was just another example of my laddish juvenilia of the time, but I have to concede there is an element of truth that effectively captures the railwaymen I remember the most. Back in the day, I had subconsciously internalised what I imagined to be typical characteristics of the average long-service railwayman – the older guys that simply 'belonged' to the works. They would usually drink in the same working man's club six or seven nights a week, and had acquired the skill of rolling their cigarettes as thin as they possibly could – almost like cocktail sticks – so that their tobacco would last for days. If you mentioned a public bar you had been in recently, the response invariably went something like, 'Good god, how much did you pay for a pint in there?' The funny thing was that if ever you had reason to go into their club, sometimes for a darts match, these guys would buy your beer for you all night long. It was then that I realised that it wasn't so much about the money; rather it was the bragging rights about how much they paid for their beer, so they were actually quite generous. Another thing they liked to brag about was how much money they had saved whenever they went away for a few days – usually during 'Trip Fortnight'. For example, when a long-service railwayman went on holiday, he generally travelled down on one of his four or five free railway passes, so the location would always be within the bounds of his travel entitlement. On arriving at his chosen destination, he would invariably spend the week with relatives or friends (quite often former or retired railmen) who would look after him much more cheaply than the seafront hotels would. Evening entertainment would again usually involve a railwayman's, ex-serviceman's or other working man's club that sold unbelievably cheap beer and pub food, and he would arrive home at the end of the week not much worse off than when he left – not withstanding which he would still find something to complain about!

I think that among some of the older guys, there seemed to be a general reluctance to engage too deeply with the modern world. A lot of these men were still going home to watch black-and-white televisions in the early 1980s! I also remember that several railmen I got to know even steered clear of opening bank accounts, preferring instead to trust their hard-earned life savings to the biscuit tin at the bottom of the wardrobe, or under the bed. I could name one railman who, upon treating himself to new car, promptly paid up with wads of banknotes fished out of a plastic supermarket bag. It was common to hear some of the older railmen bragging that they hadn't opened a wage packet for ages – one old guy I remember insisted he hadn't opened one for more than a year! 'We live off Mam's money and put mine away,' he said – it amused me that some of the older men referred to their wives as 'Mam'.

I remember other railmen who were always deeply suspicious of everything and everyone – especially when it came to money. I heard talk of one old guy who kept hold of every wage slip he had ever received for more than forty years, 'Just in case they check back,' he always used to say. Every slip was bound together using sticky tape onto a huge roll of wage slips the size of a wagon wheel leaning against the back of his tool cabinet.

More often than not inside there would be collections going around, usually on a Friday afternoon. It was apparent that so many men who had worked inside all of their lives, often in very unhealthy conditions in their earlier years, struggled to make it to retirement – meaning that many of them died or became very sick while 'in service'. If there was a collection going around, most railmen were always very generous, but you could always count on the same old faces to do a runner – head off to the lavatory when they saw the collection approaching. We used to watch them dash around to the other side of the carriage and peer beneath the coach body to see which way the collector's legs were heading, before making sure they went in the opposite direction. While still on the subject of money, few things generated more emotion in the men than the subject of overtime! Time and a half in the evenings, and on Saturdays, and then the big one – double time on Sundays. Men would stress themselves into an early grave wondering, 'Will we get our Saturday working this week?' or, 'Who would get the Sunday working this week?' I've seen the door to the chargeman's hut kicked clean off its hinges during a row over the awarding of overtime. On one occasion during those aforementioned 'one out, all out' meetings, the union called for a complete ban on overtime working, to which the assembled militants reluctantly agreed by a show of hands. I heard stories of grown men crying that day, choking back the tears as they asked their colleagues how they would survive without their overtime. I could almost feel the sense of relief when, during the early 1980s, they no longer had to worry about the overtime. This was when the management called a halt to all overtime working at a stroke – arguably a significant step on the path towards the eventual run down and closure of the works. To my mind, the men were not so much cut up about losing out on the extra money that the overtime afforded them; rather they were probably more upset by the fact that they would not know what to do with themselves on a Saturday or a Sunday morning if they could not go inside for a few hours, to the one place where most of them felt that they belonged! As I wrote earlier, many among the men freely admitted that they lived to serve the works, and in some cases, this also extended to a reluctance to take their full holiday allowance. I remember one old GWR man expressing his displeasure when the chargehand informed him he still had to take a few days' holiday owing to him, conscious of the fact that the year was fast approaching its end. The old guy flatly refused to take them, and when I jokingly said that I would use them up for him, the next moment he was rushing up the stairs to enquire about whether or not I could use up the remainder of his holiday allowance. Needless to say, that the request was refused!

If overtime was the primary obsession with certain men, then a very close second was the 'Big E', or Entitlement Day to give it its proper name. If you had ten years of continuous service you were entitled to three sick days a year with full pay. On the morning after a man had taken his 'Big E' day, he would have to get his clock card signed by a foreman to get his money made up – a process that usually involved a measure of interrogation from the said foreman. Certain men on the section would use up their full quota of E-days year in and year out, considering it to be like an addition to their holiday entitlement. Those who never qualified for E-days, or who played by the rules, would be scathing towards those that didn't, and would gather together to watch the regular 'offender' to see when he would approach the foreman. Thereafter the vitriol would kick in: 'Lazy ★★★★, he doesn't want to work and they let him get away with it … lazy ★★★★.'

There were occasions when offenders would get caught out; such stories of men spotted getting off of the train at Weymouth Station and being reported or 'snitched' to the foreman on the following Monday were almost legendary. 'Enjoy ourselves at the seaside did we?' the foreman would ask as the startled offender approached him with his clocking-in card to be signed. The offender would then sheepishly take his card back to the rack, mindful that he would be minus a day's pay the following week.

Another memorable part of that railway 'mentality' was the belief that you could either get hold of anything or get anything done on the inside. What would generally be considered in most factories as petty theft nowadays could at once be overcome by obtaining a signed chitty from a foreman. In a lot of cases the material was signed off simply as 'offcuts' or as 'surplus material'. It was a common thing at break times for a colleague to sit discussing a certain DIY project he had on the go, while the rest of the gang would break in with suggested shop or store numbers, each denoting where best to obtain the required materials. Any suggestion of buying any of the things that were needed was always met with sniggers, and sometimes roars of laughter.

As far as the paint stores was concerned, you had to be very careful agreeing to requests for paint, as there was rarely such a thing as surplus paint. If the offender was caught, the first question was usually, 'If you want to keep your job, you need to tell us who gave it to you.' I learnt this lesson very quickly when I witnessed one of my fellow coach-painters being led away by two security guards, having been named by the offender. The Glass House, the storeroom where huge sheets of glass of all thicknesses were kept, was just the same, except the men would be waving sheets of paper, upon which were written a list of dimensions to which the glass was to be cut. Again, the chitty was generally signed up as an 'off-cut', when in truth the requirement had probably been cut from a much larger sheet of glass. Every satisfied customer carrying off his sheet of glass would next arrive at No. 34 Shop for his bag of putty and glazing pins.

As in most cases, there are always characters who would take such embezzlements to the nth degree, but more often than not, such stories were a bit too tall to be believed, or were often told tongue in cheek. Could it really have been true that one particularly cheeky customer not only acquired all the materials to construct a decent-sized greenhouse in his garden but he even had the audacity to erect the building on the company premises to check for any faults or defects? No doubt all the other sections contained many similar 'treasures' that could be acquired, either by stealth or through sufficiently buttering up the section foreman. My favourite tall story from back in the day concerned a sheet metal worker who made himself a smart, galvanised metal trailer and then brazenly towed it away through the main car park entrance. No wonder it seemed to me at times that no railway worker ever actually bought anything, or feared that whatever he was doing might land him in hot water. Whatever you wanted, somebody always knew somebody who could get it for you.

Some readers might be inclined to suggest, 'Is it no wonder the Swindon Works closed with so much company material being so casually signed off as "offcuts"?' The truth is that such practices had endured for more than a century. Age-old stories were always being told of house fronts, sheds and garden lock-ups painted in chocolate and cream – those colours synonymous with the passenger coaches in the days of the Great Western Railway. It simply was not theft, provided you had a signed up chitty from a foreman. On occasions where petty theft did occur, it did indeed carry an element of risk, particularly if you happened to be one of the first employees to reach the gate on the wrong day. Usually, when the railway police were carrying out searches, word would quickly pass up the slope leading towards the gate that they were searching people. Whenever this happened, one or two would do an about-turn, and jars and packages of all shapes would suddenly be offloaded into the hedge, or rushed back inside the works to be hidden away and retrieved the next day when the coast would probably be clear. Men did occasionally get caught though, and it was often the ones who very rarely took anything. This usually meant that their houses and cars would be thoroughly searched for any further stolen items, and they would suddenly find themselves facing a suspension, or much worse depending on the scale of the offence.

When the works began to run down, particularly when the closure was imminent, the searches were relaxed, and employees could get a chitty signed for just about anything. Just about everybody walked out with a bench vice, and I remember the paint stores becoming more like a walk-around supermarket without any checkouts or store detectives. There would be an endless procession of men brandishing powdered milk tins or coffee jars of all sizes, each wanting 'a little drop of this or that'. It wasn't only paint that they were after either, as French polish, varnish, white spirit, wire wool and even paintbrushes and pallet knives were suddenly in demand.

Another taboo I remember, particularly in the Paint Shop, was the amount of time spent doing 'foreigners' – jobs for somebody else other than British Rail Engineering Ltd. The signwriters among us were always kept very busy with a collection of boards or plaques of various sizes waiting to be written. They would either be 'love jobs' (favours done for nothing) or done on the side for a small fee. Some signwriters would spend an enormous amount of time painting up historical railway plaques, nameplates or badges that had been cast on the premises. There was always a waiting list of enthusiasts requiring these to be cast and painted, and I often spent entire dinner breaks doing one or two of those collectables myself, only to be rewarded with a chocolate bar by the tight-fisted recipient. Garden gnomes and plaster animals such as squirrels and rabbits were also made on site and painted up on the section. I remember being presented with a superbly sculptured wooden animal head that was required to be varnished to perfection. This practice was not new, nor was it exclusive to the later years when discipline was a lot more lax inside the works. I was told many times of the thousands of metal soldiers that were cast and painted in the workshops ready for Christmas during the GWR days. The sons of every railway worker must have been presented with a set of these toy soldiers on every Christmas morning.

Some of the more industrious employees among the workforce, in an effort to boost their weekly earnings, would set themselves up in business by opening up a little snack shop of sorts, usually at a location adjacent to their work area. To be able to do this you first had to make sure that there were no other shops in the vicinity, and then if you wanted to do it legitimately you had to get the permission of the shop foreman. If this permission were not granted, then you would have to sell your stock covertly. This was not easy, yet there were men who got away with it for years. I remember on occasions being given directions to where I could find a shop and then upon arriving at the given location seeing no evidence of one. I then had to make further enquiries within the area to which I had been directed. A signal would be given to the 'shopkeeper', who then led me towards a seemingly normal workbench and cupboard, before proceeding to pull open the tool draws to reveal an inventory of packets of crisps all neatly stored for maximum space usage. Then he would fling open the doors of the tool cupboard to reveal a well-stocked sweetshop, at the base of which was a crude-looking refrigerator filled with cans of coke. Coach finisher Tony Rima remembered the unofficial shops in No. 24 Shop during the early 1960s:

> These shops sold most things you might need – packets of cheap tea, Beecham's Powders, sweets and even condoms! There were at least three 'shops' in 24 Shop – possibly more. There were no vending machines dispensing drinks at that time.

There were also a number of men who would sell the garden produce they had grown on their allotments to their workmates. Huge tool cupboards were filled with bags of vegetables with names written upon them, and all throughout the day men would arrive to collect the potatoes and cabbages, etc., that they had ordered – probably for a few pence cheaper than they would cost if they were purchased at the local supermarket. One good friend of mine used to make an extra few quid by selling rabbits or pheasants that he'd shot on some local farmer's land. He was forever receiving complaints that the meat was filled with lead shot, often causing the recipient to break his teeth. Sometimes we would be sat there in our gang hut during tea break when, during a lull in the conversation, one could suddenly hear the flicking sounds of trapped fleas jumping around inside the bags in which the promised rabbits were being kept.

There were other little favours that could be done for the purpose of securing an extra few bob. Some men could make a few extra pennies by getting the morning papers for the entire gang each day to save everyone the bother of interrupting their journey to work. Almost everyone inside would read *The Sun*, *The Daily Mail* or *The Daily Mirror* depending on their political persuasion. Other employees would boost their income by selling such things as Moonraker weekly draw tickets or Swindon Town scratch cards or pools coupons, etc. Some elderly employees seemed to spend their entire day pushing their bike around the factory peddling these kinds of games. Then, as I mentioned earlier, there were the 'porn merchants' who would supply or swap whatever magazines they had available. When the video age kicked in, these same employees were able to extend their businesses significantly. Quite often as an effective means of picking up a nice little bonus, the porn merchants would put on a show at somebody's house (usually one of the single chaps) and charge a small fee to everyone wishing to attend. It amused me to hear that ham or cheese rolls were usually laid on at an additional charge.

It would appear from most of what I had written all those years ago that the senior GWR guys were often given a hard time by the younger men in the various departments. This probably had a lot to do with them having avoided past headcount reductions on account of their longer service. When I look back today, I often think that many of those former GWR men were never afforded the respect that was due to them. This was the late 1970s to early 1980s when many veterans of the Second World War were still of working age. I'm now thinking of men I knew and worked with, and who had spent many days, or even weeks of their young lives floating on life rafts after their seagoing vessels had been torpedoed by enemy U-boats. I also listened intently to the recollections of colleagues who were machine gunned while running between foxholes – and proudly showed me their bullet scars to prove it. There were also men who for many months had been prisoners in Burma; to watch these men eating their food at break times was to watch men who had known real hunger. It was noticeable that many of these men avoided recounting their experiences, and even as a young lad I knew that it would be quite wrong or inappropriate of me to press them for one could see that the suffering they had endured never really left their faces. In contrast, it appeared that those who were forced to endure National Service, or 'the mob' as they always called it during the 1950s, never seemed to stop talking about it, despite the fact that they had never experienced front-line warfare, nor heard a single shot fired in anger. They would constantly lament the fact that National Service had been curtailed long before us bunch of 'hairy urchins' could be similarly forced to endure the same measure of discipline and humiliation. For those men who had genuinely been wounded to the point of disablement during their military service, the company afforded them the right to clock off a few minutes earlier to give them the opportunity to get ahead of the crowd.

For reasons that would give the modern health and safety officer a brain seizure, Christmases were also very memorable in the Swindon Works. Despite the annual notices that went up every year warning that alcohol was not to be consumed on the premises, the last working day before Christmas was always party time, often involving some not so covert drinking. Almost every workplace cabin table was adorned with Wadsworth Party Sevens or Party Fours and occasionally someone would produce a bottle of whisky. Added to this were platefuls of cakes, mince pies, crisps, etc. – all laid out, of course, on the obligatory blue industrial tissue paper. Some foremen would generally turn a blind eye to the blatant disregarding of the rules in relation to boozing, and some would even drop by for a quick tipple and a chat. When the order to clock out was finally received around lunchtime, the clubs and bars surrounding the factory were full to bursting point with very high-spirited railwaymen. Malcolm Holland (1979 intake) remembered one such occasion:

> My first Christmas in the works (1980), I was with the maintenance gang somewhere in the middle of A Shop. The charge man had a bottle of the hard stuff in his cabin which he handed round the gang on the morning before we finished for Christmas – drinking at work! Imagine that now!
>
> Of all the places I have worked in my life, those Christmases at the works stand out the most. After finishing my time and working on the 19 Shop lift-roads we all chipped in a little extra into the 'tea club' so we could all go out for a pie and a pint or two at The Glue Pot after we finished at lunchtime on Christmas Eve. Simple pleasures, but fondly remembered.

These Christmas Eve parties were a long-standing tradition, even going back to the days when workers were only given Christmas Day and Boxing Day off, as coach finisher Tony Rima remembered:

> The Majority of the men stopped work after lunch on Christmas Eve and had parties, with only a few of the men working on. I remember one apprentice going to the pub at lunchtime and returning with two bottles of sherry, one of which he downed in one go. To say he was drunk would be an understatement!

Having spent the remainder of my working life in manufacturing, I do look back to these days and am firmly of the opinion that some things have changed for the better. By that I mean certain practices that can no longer be passed off as 'just factory life' or a means to alleviate the 'earthiness and monotony of the manual workers daily life' (as Hugh Freebury had put it). I learned very early on in my time inside that you had to be able to take a joke. You either had to laugh along with it, or find some other way of turning the tables on the joker. Put simply – you daren't let the practical joker 'get to you'. There were men who could not take a joke, a position that laid them wide open to being targeted by show-offs purely to get laughs. Bullying was not rife in Swindon Works, but it did happen. The men who were targeted were usually either weak characters or sometimes just too cheeky or too vocal for their own good. I've seen grown men in floods of tears after having their arms twisted tightly behind their backs – an uncomfortable thing for a fresh-faced apprentice to have to witness. Such a thing would be unimaginable in the workplace today, yet these occurrences were laughed off as a joke by other gang members while the humiliated men, drying their eyes in some cases, would tend to their painful joints. Sometimes it would be the tickling treatment – a lot less painful, but still a humiliating experience for the recipient as he fought to escape from the clutches of his assailant. These kinds of things did not happen every week, nor did they happen every month. The fact remains that I witnessed incidents that went a lot further than mere 'horseplay' on several occasions, and it made a strong impression upon me. I never expected to see men who were at work to earn a living being humiliated like downtrodden schoolboys!

Why was this allowed to happen? I think the decades that had rolled by since the days of the GWR had not only brought about changes in working practices but also the demise of discipline. To a large degree, the institutionalised railwayman mentality had gradually given over to a more general 'factory mentality' of the kind that had been forged in an era of union-led, shop floor militancy. It is probably fair to say that by the time I had completed my apprenticeship, and the first rumblings of trouble on the horizon were being felt, the levels of discipline, of which those who had gone before me have since written, had largely broken down. Employees rarely got 'called up on the carpet' (as it was known) to explain themselves. It became increasingly common to see a man having a stand-up row with his foreman on the shop floor; such behaviour merely added to the fall off in standards. One former railman, Percy Warwick, said he felt that, 'It all went downhill when you started calling foremen by their first names – it wasn't like that in the good old days.'[47]

Managers and foremen generally turned a blind eye to less painful humiliations of the 'all in good fun type', such as the ball and chain treatment. On the Friday before a man was due to be married, he would be pinned down while a heavy ball and chain was attached to his leg. Thereafter he would be paraded around the shop floor while his colleagues aimed fire hoses at him. I suffered this particular humiliation myself on the final day before my wedding, and went home thoroughly drenched. On other sections the rituals were somewhat different, and if the things I overheard were true, they were certainly a lot worse than the ball and chain treatment!

On a lighter note, there were other instances of horseplay that everybody looked forward to. This usually occurred when a gang member was late. As soon as the clock ticked five or six minutes past the starting time, every other gang member would arm themselves with the heaviest or noisiest item they could find. When the sheepish latecomer approached the clocking bay the 'fanfare' started; the most fearful racket was made as these objects were bashed against the benches and metal cabinets. If it was a regular latecomer, the fanfare was never likely to be quite so bad, but if it was someone who was rarely late, he usually got the full treatment right throughout the 'walk of shame' to his coat locker. This had been a long-standing tradition in the works for decades. Bob Gale remembered this ritual from the 1950s in the AE Shop: 'The banging on the sides of locos or other metal objects was quite a good deterrent to make you be at work on time – for a few weeks at least!'

Finally, I cannot leave off from citing examples of horseplay without remembering the prank that involved painting the back of somebody's shoe heels while they stood chatting to a colleague, completely unaware of course. In his book *Great Western Apprentice: Swindon in the Thirties,* Hugh Freebury wrote up an account of this prank going on in the 1930s! A pair of fitters known as 'The Terrible Twins' became notorious for the mischief they caused and the pranks they played:

> One would engage a workman or an apprentice in conversation near the edge of an engine pit, while his fellow conspirator down below painted the heels of his boots with red lead paint or whitening.

Eventually the men got wise to this and stood well far of the pit when in conversation. Not to be outdone, they started attaching the paint brush to a long broom handle. During my time, this prank was generally exclusive to the painting sections, with the idea being to 'get' the highest-profile target possible. If you managed to get a foreman's heels, that was an impressive trophy indeed. If you got a manager's heels, you were then without a doubt considered to be the absolute kingpin of the section. One heel on its own didn't count – you had to get them both to take the honours. Jim Toolen remembered this prank:

> I remember having my heels painted silver by someone down in the pits in the A Shop, and then the calling of Yee-ha as to the 'spurs' you were wearing. Extra brownie points if you got a chargehand.

Nigel Hobbs remembers other pranks that were often played on apprentices or 'fresh meat' as they were often referred:

> In No. 6 Shop we would 'tail' an apprentice with a long strip of blue paper towel – sometimes setting it alight. Sometimes apprentices went home looking like flour-graders, totally covered in French chalk. How many of us carried around the 'happy-slap' pink handprints on the backs of our overalls from the pink barrier cream?

6

THE BEGINNING OF THE END

From the day I had begun my association with British Rail in the summer of 1977, I don't think I ever fully shrugged off the weight of insecurity – the feeling that I had entered into an occupation in which the long-term future was always open to speculation. This was despite Harry Roberts, the Works Manager, having assured us new apprentices that he had resolved to go against the recommendation of his employers and would keep the workshops open. With those words still ringing in my ears, I transferred over to the works a year later, feeling as though I had climbed aboard the BREL express under a clear blue sky – save for a few dark clouds on the horizon that seemed to be getting less dark by the day. In the turbulence-free years that followed, I had been able to complete my apprenticeship and been re-employed as a tradesman coach painter before the storm clouds began to gather once more. Those clouds had become much darker by the early 1980s, when even the most optimistic among us had seriously begun to fear for our jobs as once more the workforce became haunted by the fear of unemployment. Throughout the early 1980s our daily lives became a constant vacillation between feelings of hope and moods of despair. One dared to feel optimistic when the workshops looked full, a state of mind that could swiftly evolve into a more pessimistic outlook when the internal tracks began to look bare again. These ever-changing emotions were the hallmark of those final years leading up to eventual closure.

Surprisingly there had been no real resurgence of any serious doubts about the future survival of the works when Margaret Thatcher had come to power in 1979. She had triumphed on a ticket that advocated a programme of privatisation for some of Britain's key nationalised industries – a policy that clearly would not have been a good thing for employees of BREL and the Swindon workforce in particular. Initial fears among the men over what might happen were quickly dispelled by the award of a substantial two-tier, inflation-busting pay increase during her first year in power. Nobody mentioned anything about 'looking a gift horse in the mouth', and why would they? Just a few months prior to the election, the Swindon Works had been awarded a huge contract to overhaul the entire Southern Region commuter train fleet. This work was scheduled to start arriving immediately, beginning with the Kent Coast, short-haul fleet, which meant that the works began recruiting furiously on a massive scale. The local paper wrote of a 'Jobs Bonanza' at Swindon Works, indicating that more than 1,000 workers would have to be recruited over the next eighteen months.[48] This contract required British Rail to pump more than £3 million into the facility to keep the ageing machinery up to scratch, and had negated any need for redundancies for a number of years. Little wonder there were many employees in the works who were happy to admit they would vote Conservative, despite accusations of being 'working-class Tories stabbing themselves in the back'. Many of these men had been made redundant under a previous Labour government in the 1960s and had little faith in the widely held belief that the Labour Party was the party for the working class.

The Southern Region contract had been viewed as yet another triumph for Harry Roberts, who asserted his determination that the works would honour its new commitments. And yet, despite such a massive shot in the arm for the facility, some workers still considered the contract to be a mere stopgap for two or three years, and never tired of resurrecting the likelihood of mass redundancies and closure. 'They've taken on too many too soon,' you would hear people say; 'It won't be long before they have to send them all back down the slope.' Redundancy was always referred to as 'going down the slope', as in, 'We're all going down the slope.' I heard that phrase repeated maybe a dozen times a day during those final years, usually with an F-word thrown in for good measure. 'The slope', or 'the slippery slope' as it was sometimes called, referred to the slope at the beginning of the main tunnel exit in London Street.

By the beginning of 1982 Harry Roberts had long since retired. He had, in fairness, kept his word and the workshops had remained open and even prospered to a considerable degree under his watch. Even though much idle speculation about the future of the works had continued, people generally felt more secure while Roberts was at the helm. Even he probably knew deep down that he had merely bought the works some time, and that there was always a 'bigger picture' – a longer-term plan that would not include Swindon Works. Now that Roberts was gone, and a new Works Manager was in place, the workforce could no longer fall back on the genuine sincerity in his words for any comfort. He had always had great faith in the skilled craftsmen at Swindon Works, especially their particular ability to deliver on time any orders that came their way even in the most difficult circumstances. Following his retirement, Harry Roberts reflected on the period when the contract for the twenty Hunslet Shunting Locomotives for Kenya was agreed. He admitted that his colleagues considered him 'crazy to have taken it on', and yet the contract was delivered in record-breaking time at tender price, just as the first Swindon locomotive, the *Great Western*, had been in 1846. Shortly before the works closed, Roberts paid this glowing tribute to the Swindon workforce:[49]

> Swindon had built no locomotives for thirteen years, were flat-footed from the start – no jigs, no materials and no staff! The common factor in both instances was the superb quality and dedication of the Swindon craftsmen, and I am very proud of the fact that for nearly a decade I had the privilege of working with such men as their Works Manager.

Today, there appears to be a measure of cynicism among the older veterans of Swindon Works when they look back to this period of the works' history. One foreman from the AE Shop, who preferred to stay anonymous, told me that he felt many people in power already knew Swindon only had ten years, even after Harry Roberts had arrived:

> There's a lot of talk about Harry Roberts having succeeded in reviving the works, but a lot of people already knew we only had ten years. They [BR] just threw us a few scraps now and then just to keep us going. Most of the work was rubbish!

Rubbish some of it might have been, but at that time any new order was welcomed as a shot in the arm – even if it was just a few wagons. Throughout the 'Roberts era' Swindon Works had taken full advantage of government legislation from 1968 that allowed railway workshops to compete for non-railway work. We serviced sawmill engines for Africa, redesigned buses, serviced vintage car gearboxes and marine Maybach engines, built high-speed offshore boats, ship's hatches, missile launchers, torpedo parts, hospital trolleys and turntables.

> Swindon never said no – neither could she afford to be selective, so the majority of unpopular work tended to gravitate towards Swindon. There were no demarcation and manning problems, meaning that management could commit to a growth strategy.
>
> Harry Roberts, 1985

It was a growth strategy that had triggered a considerable rise in the headcount at the works during Roberts' tenure. It was noticeable that even after he had retired the 'unpopular' work continued to find its way into Swindon Works. At one point during the run down Swindon was given an order to build a small consignment of nuclear flask wagons for the Central Electricity Generating Board (CEGB). The first of the wagons was completed in 1984 and subjected to a stringent testing process before a specially assembled gathering of press and an additional 1,500 invited guests. The 50-ton flask was filled with pressurised water and steel bars to simulate the spent Magnox nuclear fuel rods it was designed to carry, and then laid horizontally across the track. A diesel locomotive with three carriages was crashed into the wagon at 90mph; when the dust settled, aside from a few bent fins it was plain to see that, to the delight of the CEGB, the expertise of the Swindon workers had passed the test. The wagons thereafter covered more than 6 million miles in 14,000 separate journeys to the nuclear reprocessing plant at Sellafield, problem free.[50]

Throughout the first few months of 1982, hardly a week went by without at some point work grinding to a halt while those present got stuck into a long, drawn-out conversation about the future of the works. It was usually

The contract to build six atomic flask wagons became one of the final orders for the works. (Tony Rima Collection)

triggered by a baseless rumour or a little bit of leg-pulling somewhere that had got out of hand. This was mainly because another trait common to Swindon's railwaymen was that they always seemed to rather enjoy painting the blackest picture possible, and could very easily leave you feeling quite depressed. I had very little interest in the activities of trade unions (even though I was a member of one), and on occasions when those chaotic mass meetings took place to discuss the situation, I first had to discover from those closer to the front what exactly was said, and then chew it over in my mind, but I never really got too involved. After all, it was not that long since I had been 'the boy', a subspecies whose opinions were not generally given much credence!

As time went by, despite the tide of rumour-spreading and baseless gossip about how 'grim' our outlook appeared to be, I simply refused to put my life on hold just to wait and see what might or might not happen. I had got married in 1981, bought my first house in 1981 and then started a family inside two years, so for me the stakes gradually became much higher

Shop meetings on the A Shop traversing table became a regular occurrence in the early 1980s. (Andy Binks, The Swindon Society)

whenever the future of the works came up for discussion. I still remember too well when I proudly announced that my wife was expecting our first child that, while some of the men congratulated me warmly, others suggested some various ways of 'solving the problem' owing to the perilous circumstances. Factory banter I know, but some men never got tired of reminding those of us getting on with our lives that we were wasting our time because, ultimately, 'We were all going down the slope!'

The rumour mill gathered at a pace because a lot of railmen who had previously fallen victim to redundancy had long memories and knew the signs to look out for. They also knew the kinds of underhand tricks that were sometimes pulled for the purpose of self-preservation. Many of the men I now worked among had been victims of the 'last in, first out' policy and knew they would fall victim to the same rule again at the next sign of trouble. It is often forgotten that another of the common characteristics of men who felt they *belonged* to the works was that the redundant former employees always came back again. There was never any question that when things looked up again, back they would come like bees to a hive. One could detect a clear measure of resentment from these men towards the older ex-GWR hands who had always managed to avoid being affected by severe headcount reductions, men who had led a relatively sheltered working life beneath the comfortable blanket of their long service. Time and again you would hear, 'This place has been bloody good to the likes of them,' whenever past redundancies were discussed. This time around the 'last in, first out' policy would be problematical, mainly because there had been so much redeployment over the year that it was difficult to gauge who was ahead of who when it came to the crunch. Very soon one noticed that certain men would disappear off the section for secretive meetings with their union representative to ensure that their official position in the pecking order tied in with their own understanding.

Pride in the job! Typically, throughout those perilous final years a lot of the men just put their worries aside, preferring to just get on with the job in the same way they had done for decades. (Tony Rima Collection)

As things turned out, it was the events of April 1982 that would mark the beginning of the end during that final chapter of Swindon Works. Word had got out that a big meeting was being held at the British Rail headquarters in Euston where the future role of each of the thirteen BREL workshops was to be discussed. As early as 14 April a delegation from Swindon had gone to London to meet with representatives from other workshops to state Swindon's position. Even before the meeting had begun, the contingent from Swindon had been rocked by a formal announcement from British Rail that all apprentice recruitment at Swindon was to be axed. The Works Training School situated in Newburn Crescent was to be mothballed until further notice. At a meeting in Derby that day, BR bosses were insistent that, 'Owing to the workload situation it is no longer considered prudent to take on any more youngsters.'[51] Union Leaders were quick to respond, highlighting the serious problem of youth unemployment locally, and called upon youth project officials in the town to demand that the decision be reversed and that the Work's Training School be kept open. The Work's Committee were equally angry that the decision had also been taken to sell off the apprentice hostel in Bath Road, a facility remembered fondly by many hundreds of outstation apprentices that had served the Western Region since 1961.

As things turned out, 1981–82 did indeed see the final full complement of 100 apprentices coming into the Works Training School. However, for reasons that never became clear, further 'Swindon apprentices' were accepted into the school for the years 1982–83 (fifty-two apprentices) and 1983–84 (forty-four). Some of these lads had initially been offered apprenticeships, but the offer was withdrawn and replaced by an offer to begin training on a Youth Opportunities Programme. The 1984–85 intake contained twenty outstation BR apprentices, along with a small number of Youth Training Scheme (YTS) lads who were able to go over to Swindon Works to gain some additional training before the closure. BR outstation apprentices were still being accepted at the school in the year 1985–86 before completing their apprenticeships at their home depot. Looking through some of the training records, it is apparent that in November 1985 a small number of apprentices were transferred over to British Leyland at the Pressed Steel Fisher plant in Swindon to complete their apprenticeships.

So it appears that at some point in the proceedings, the BR board relented and allowed two further intakes of apprentices into the Works Training School who were destined for Swindon Works. Maybe the persuasive efforts of David Stoddart MP had achieved a measure of success with his negotiations on this issue? Ryan Conduit, who entered the Works Training School as a YTS first-year apprentice in 1982, and became the final apprentice to 'come out of his time' at Swindon Works, provides us with an interesting alternative explanation as to why he thinks this might have happened:

> I remember at around the time I completed my first year of training, my father (an engine driver) came home from work to be told by my mother, 'I have been talking to your boss this afternoon.' My dad thought she meant his manager, but No! My mother had spent two hours on the phone to Sir Peter Parker, Chairman of the British Railways Board. She explained to him that the town of Swindon had been born as a result of the railways, and by killing off apprenticeships he was not investing in the future.
>
> What I can say is that he thanked her and said he would personally look into this. Mum did get a letter back from Sir Peter in which he thanked her and said that 'as long as there is a railworks in Swindon it would continue to train apprentices right to the end'. Thereafter us YTS lads were suddenly taken on as full apprentices. I'm not saying my mother changed Sir Peter's mind, but something turned 180 degrees after that phone call.

Ryan was not the only first-year apprentice to benefit from this sudden change of heart:

> I was offered an apprenticeship in 1982. It was then withdrawn and I started training at Dean Street on a Youth Opportunities Programme. After completing the YOP the top twenty or so were then offered apprenticeships.

Adi Phillips, 1982 intake

The big meeting at Rail House took place on 22 April 1982. The 100-plus placard-waving Swindon contingent who descended on London that day had already been primed to expect an announcement of a minimum of 204 job losses at the works. This would be made up mainly from apprentices who had come out of their time, so to speak, not being kept on. Employee representatives, already angry at the announcement that all apprentice recruitment would be curtailed, did not hide their fears that the situation could be about to get much worse. Some considered it to be potentially the biggest threat the works had ever faced, indicating that the job losses announced that day could be anything from the initial 204 already known upwards to complete closure of the works. The plan for the day was to march from Paddington to Euston to lobby the meeting of BR management and unions, and then a representative body would continue on to the House of Commons to lobby MPs. They would be joined by representatives from other BREL workshops, who were equally worried about being on a possible hit list.

When it finally came, the blow that was struck at the meeting was far more severe than any of the demonstrators from around the country had seriously imagined. The BR board announced that the Swindon workforce, currently running at more than 3,500, would have to be reduced to around 2,000 – a figure it hoped to achieve without the need for any compulsory redundancies. The figure quoted at the meeting was 1,293 redundancies – 448 to go by the end of 1982, with a further 845 to be released by the end of December 1983 on completion of the Southern Rail electrical multiple unit refurbishment contract. Plans were also announced to switch shunting locomotive repairs from Swindon to Doncaster, Eastleigh and Glasgow. The only chink of light for the Swindon Works was the transfer of non-passenger rolling stock repairs from York, Wolverton and Doncaster to Swindon. BR also announced the closures of Temple Mills Works in Greater London and Horwich Works in Lancashire by the end of 1983, and, the biggest shock of all, that Shildon Wagon Works in County Durham would be run down in 1983 with a view to closure in 1984. This collection of closures amounted to the loss of a further 3,566 jobs.

The BREL management followed up the announcement with a special issue of its corporate flyer *Railtalk* in which it outlined its problems in a question and answer format. The chief problem was stated as being that BREL no longer had sufficient new construction, maintenance or repair work to justify the continued retention of the twelve main works. The problems were outlined in further detail in answer to another question:

> The continuing drive by BR for more competitive performance rests heavily on better utilisation of all assets. The introduction of the High Speed Train and more intensive use of other locomotives, multiple units and carriages have resulted in a significant reduction in fleet sizes.

In answer to the question of why the axe had fallen so heavily on Shildon, Horwich and Swindon, BREL stated that the focus had been on 'certain operating expenses' that could not be reduced, and were now impacting on product prices, increases that could only be met by increased passenger and freight revenue.

> The only way of reducing these costs is by disposing of the under-utilised surplus workshop capacity. The measures proposed will save an estimated £50m[illion] between 1983 and 1986, and another £18m[illion] per annum thereafter.

Things could have been so different if the government of the day had followed a prescribed programme of investment, rather than one of starving the industry of cash. Having been all too fond of avoiding any responsibility for any decisions affecting British Rail ('these decisions are for British Rail'), it soon became clear that the Thatcher government, already presiding over a deep economic recession, had flatly refused to approve the further investment required to bring Britain's railways up to scratch. In the year prior to the first wave of job cuts at Swindon, the annual investment expenditure of British Rail had fallen from £513 million in 1979 to £333 million in 1981.[52] At the beginning of the 1980s Sir Peter Parker, Chairman of BR, had issued what was effectively a blueprint for the revival of Britain's railways throughout the decade. Sir Peter explained that government funding was seriously inadequate, and that routes on the fringes faced imminent closure if the monetary squeeze was not relaxed. He pointed to the 800 miles of outstanding track renewals, coupled with another 300 miles of severe speed restrictions, and famously described the situation as, 'The crumbling edge of quality.' The government felt that BR could achieve much greater efficiency, even though it was already the second most cost-effective rail network in Europe after Sweden.

Sir Peter went on to propose a massive electrification of the system, along with a widespread expansion in rolling stock and track, a Channel tunnel link, a cross-London link, and the development of the ill-fated Advanced Passenger Train. It was estimated that the total cost of the package would amount to £1 billion by 1990. After a four-year campaign Sir Peter had at last received approval from the Ministry of Transport for his electrification proposals, only to be thwarted by Alan Walters, the Prime Minister's chief economic advisor and champion of monetarism, who queried whether the programme of expansion was commercially sound. This objection effectively delayed any decision and it was finally decided that each electrification project would be judged on strictly commercial terms. It was during these considerations that the Centre for Policy Studies, an influential think tank for the Prime Minister, published a pamphlet advocating the conversion of railways into roads, thus saving the taxpayer £1 billion a year. Thereafter the Treasury kicked the various electrification projects submitted by British Rail into the long grass. Sir Peter could not even get approval for electrification of a 27-mile stretch on the east coast main line – let alone on major routes between cities. It was felt that the government had been hostile to Sir Peter from the outset, owing to his having stood as a Labour Party candidate during the 1950s. When it finally decided to commission a review of rail finances, the government remained unreceptive towards any British Rail involvement, and no money for electrification would be made available until long after Sir Peter's retirement in 1983.[53]

So it seemed that without sufficient government investment forthcoming, BR had decided that the ideal solution to its business problem was to sack a huge number of its dedicated workforce. At around 6 p.m. on 22 April, the employees, union leaders and workers' representatives boarded their trains that would take them back to their respective works, following the day's demonstrations. As they settled into their seats, the 6 o'clock news announced the closures and mass redundancies at BREL to the nation. The furious representatives and employees who had descended on Euston and Westminster that day would begin drawing up their battle plans the following day. All resolved that they would fight the cuts and closures to the death.

7

A FIGHT TO THE DEATH

Of the workshops that had been targeted by BREL on that infamous day, the axe had fallen particularly heavy on Shildon, Horwich and Swindon. The question on every employee representative's mind was, 'Do we fight the cuts collectively, or do we fight tooth and nail in an effort to save our own works?' Suddenly, every union official and workers' representative had to think very carefully about how they would respond when questioned about how they would fight the cuts and, in Swindon's case, about what they needed to do to protect the remaining 2,000 jobs. It could be argued that the management of BREL encouraged a measure of divide and rule by seemingly picking off one workshop at a time. Maybe this time they also hoped that a degree of self-preservation would come into play – leaving the doomed workshops to fight their battles alone.

This is essentially what happened during the first few months following the announcement. A plan for representatives of all the affected works to lobby MPs at Westminster again was at first organised by representatives from Swindon and Horwich to take place sometime in May. Then at short notice, they informed the other works that they had withdrawn their participation on an agreed date of 25 May. On the day in question, only a small number of employees from Swindon and Horwich joined the 600 workers from Shildon who set off that morning from Darlington in eleven specially chartered railway carriages. They would discover on arrival in London that they would be fighting to save their existence bereft of any significant nationwide support. The Swindon Works Committee Chairman Danny Lee was adamant that Swindon had to protect itself at the expense of other workshops if it was to have a future.

It is likely that the open style of management cultivated during Harry Robert's tenure as Works Manager had a bearing on the decision to go it alone in the fight to save Swindon. When unions up and down the country were being continually engaged in what Roberts described as 'infantile squabbles', the rival unions and Works Committee representatives in Swindon actually took a more measured view of whatever situation occurred, and tended to work with management, rather than against them: 'At Swindon we had developed a management/union relationship which was light years ahead of anyone else's. We had disagreements, but these were always resolved in an adult atmosphere through logical discussions.'[54]

It would become clear in the coming months that the 'special relationship' that had existed between management and unions went out of the door with Harry Roberts, and was never going to be repeated by his replacement. Another thing that also worked in the BREL management's favour was the level of inter-union rivalry, not only within the affected plants, but also among the three major unions in general. Swindon tended to be split in half between the Transport and General Workers Union and the National Union of Railwaymen, while many of the electricians in the works were allied to the Electrical, Electronic, Telecommunications and Plumbing Union (EETPU). Other plants had long histories of inter-union rivalry, but at Swindon it never really went beyond competing for new members. However, whenever the train divers' union ASLEF flexed its muscles, the knock-on effect could not help but impact upon members of the other unions – meaning that relations between the bigger unions in particular were always strained. In May 1982 the *Daily Mirror* reported on the bitter rivalry between the two biggest rail unions NUR and ASLEF that almost resulted in a punch-up at an explosive TUC meeting in May 1982:

> ASLEF President Derek Fullick threatened to 'put one on' NUR leader Sid Weighall. TUC General Secretary Len Murray called for order, to which Mr Fullick told him, 'I'll pick you up by the braces and drop you down the lift shaft.'[55]

And this during a 'unified fight' against a 3 per cent pay offer! Not the ideal state of relations before going into battle to try and save a few thousand jobs!

From the moment the job cuts were announced, the employees' representatives resolved not to take the hammer blow lying down, and called on all employees to demonstrate their disgust. Swindon's plan of action would be coordinated first by the Joint Works Committee and then alongside the Railworks Defence Committee. The headline on the following morning's local paper stated firmly and categorically that it would be 'A fight to the death', and that the battle plans were already being drawn up to fight the proposed cuts announced on 22 April. A mass meeting of the entire workforce was called for the following Wednesday, 28 April. Acting Works Committee Chairman Terry Larkham described the decision as being 'Disastrous for the railway industry, for Swindon Works and for the whole town', and was already proposing a mass protest march of employees through the town centre.

The announcement had come exactly ten years after the last major battle to save the works following the appointment of Harry Roberts as Works Manager. The local press also went on the attack; the *Evening Advertiser* described that Thursday as 'One of the blackest days the town of Swindon had ever known'. As the full extent became clear the paper suggested in its editorial that this could be 'The beginning of the end for the Swindon Works: Swindon Works could be wiped off the map, with only the museum to remind us of the past. Closure will shake Swindon from its foundations, and maybe even the statue of Isambard Kingdom Brunel will fall from its plinth and smash into a million fragments'.[56]

Even at this early stage there was more bad news to come. On the day following the meeting, British Rail belatedly announced that the figures released to union officials on the previous day only related to shop-floor workers. It did not include 223 office and supervisory staff – meaning the total number was now 1,516 redundancies – a figure that it was claimed amounted to almost half of the current workforce.[57] Thereafter, unions informed the workforce that nothing short of total commitment to a fight would prevent closure; they accused the BR Management of effectively 'chopping the works in half'. Alan Rees, the then Works Committee Chair, spoke out in disbelief at what had happened:

> We had allowed as many as 100 voluntary redundancies to go ahead in previous weeks, despite disapproval from union head office officials, this in the belief that it would safeguard the future of the works. Craft retraining had been organised throughout the works and Swindon became a model. Now I believe they have taken the loyalty of the workforce in Swindon and abused it. It's a devastating blow. Every member of that works must feel they've been let down.

Also on 28 April, further 'battle plans' were drawn up by the Works Committee in an effort to fight the planned redundancies. A nine-point proposal was agreed, beginning with a stated intention to stop parts of Swindon's workload being transferred to other works. It was decided to seek meetings with other unions, including the train drivers' union ASLEF, in an effort to stop this movement of work from happening. An additional proposal sought to urge Thamesdown Council to refuse planning permission for any of the redundant workshops to be either torn down or used for any other purpose than railway work. Aside from vowing to maintain pressure and increase lobbying where it was needed, the Works Committee also sought an urgent meeting with the BR board over its decision to axe the Works Training School and sell off the apprentice hostel. A levy of 5p per week was requested from every union member in an effort to build up a 'fighting fund', and shop stewards were encouraged to hold regular meetings to coordinate action in the various departments. This last proposal was intended to stave off any attempts the company might make at coercing the workers into cooperating with the reorganisation plan. On the following day, the National Executive of the 170,000-strong National Union of Railwaymen passed a resolution whereby they would refuse outright to accept neither any compulsory redundancies, nor any workshop closures across the BREL network. Also that day, the town's MP David Stoddart had met with BR bosses in an effort to make them rethink proposals to close the Works Training School. It was suggested that the Manpower Services Commission (MSC) could take over the running of the school and ensure that engineering training was continued in Swindon in the interests of any future demand for skilled engineers.

The first great act of defiance occurred when a mass rally was staged in early May 1982. 'We have shouted our mouths off that this is going to be the biggest demonstration the town has ever seen, and we are going to be right,' claimed Works Committee man Harold Sealey.[58] He was indeed proved right when thousands of workers gathered at the West Gate entrance at the commencement of the afternoon shift at 1.30 p.m. Thereafter they proceeded past Farringdon Road Park, along Farnsby Street, Princess Street, past AUEW House and back towards Farringdon Road Park. The local paper reported that the demonstrators filled the whole of Commercial Road, bringing traffic to a standstill. On this occasion a very large percentage of the workforce – more than 3,000 in total – had marched along the said route to protest against the planned job cuts. Some of the men had built coffins to carry along with them as a manner of expressing their fears. A brass band led the marching army of railwaymen, who were also armed with hundreds of banners and placards, and they received wild applause from shopkeepers and traders who had lined up all along the 2-mile route in a show of support. In the press conference that preceded the march, it was pointed out that the wage bill for Swindon Works was in excess of £350,000 a week, with most of that being spent in local shops and businesses.[59] The clear message was that a lot was at stake here, not just the jobs of the marching railway workers, all of whom feared that the scale of the planned job cuts would be a giant step on the way to closure.

Over the next few months the workforce was gradually thinned out in line with the management plans. Most of the senior men in the Paint Shop opted for early redundancy – which triggered an endless round of goodbyes. Hardly a week went past without another friendly old face coming around to make his tearful farewell, and it was apparent that most of these men had known no other life outside the works, aside from their war service. I really felt for these men, and couldn't even begin to imagine what it must have felt like – walking out through the tunnel for the last time after almost fifty years working inside. We waved our GWR veterans out the door and kept our heads down, hoping for a period of calm and maybe another contract or two. At the backs of our minds, we were more than a little suspicious that the worst was yet to come.

In the months that followed the announcement, the fight to save the rail engineering jobs struggled to remain in the spotlight when it was upstaged by much bigger problems in the rail industry in the summer of 1982. The two-week strike by train drivers against the imposition of flexible rostering – the longest action in fifty-five years – had cost British Rail another £150 million. If anyone felt things could not get any worse, there was more bad news for the industry in the first weeks of the new year. Barely a few days

May 1982 and Swindon railwaymen set off on the biggest march the town had ever seen. (Tony Rima Collection)

after those major redundancies had been announced at Swindon Works, a commission of enquiry, set up by the Secretary of State for Transport to examine possible ways of improving railway finances and operations, had sat for the first time. The special enquiry, known as the Serpell Review, was backed by both the Thatcher government and the British Railways Board. The year 1982 had been the low point of a steady period of decline in passenger numbers stretching back to 1957. Revenues had decreased by £500 million over the past twelve years, while costs had risen by £200 million during the same period.[60] The BR board had been bracing themselves for recommendations for new investment towards being able to redress the balance. However, to their consternation, when the report was finally published in January 1983 it rejected the idea of further rail investment and instead focused on scope to economise. The Serpell Review was soon being touted as 'Beeching Axe II' – ironically the report's author Sir David Serpell had been on the BR board charged with putting into effect Beeching's proposals. He recommended that BR needed to cut costs by £220 million by 1986, and that the present 11,000 route miles should be reduced to 9,000 – with the fare structure being reviewed to allow for substantial increases. The report also sent further shockwaves through the rail industry by suggesting that a rail network of just 1,630 miles was the largest it considered to be viable without subsidy.[61]

Workers exit through the London Street tunnel entrance haunted by the fear of unemployment. (*Swindon Advertiser*)

Aside from recommending severe cuts in the railway network, the report also criticised the relationship between the BR board and BREL, and made further recommendations in respect of future cost reductions. Engineering accounted for just over half of British Rail's costs (£1,400 million) in 1981, and by rationalising maintenance operations by reducing the number of depots from 150 to just 20 it would save BR around £25 million a year. It was also stated that maintenance and repair costs would rise by a further £20 million over the next five years if BR did not switch its emphasis to investing in new build in an effort to reduce the average age of the fleet. For Swindon Works, exclusively a repair and refurbishment facility, this recommendation amounted to pure poison. Thereafter, Serpell spared his hottest coals for British Rail's policy of providing BREL with a virtual monopoly for supplying, repairing and refurbishing its rolling stock – this despite a declared policy of purchasing abroad whenever it was deemed commercially advantageous. How, it asked, could British Rail ever reap the benefits of worldwide competition? The report went on to criticise BR for being over-optimistic with regard to future demand – meaning it had allowed BREL to employ too many staff and to train too many new apprentices that were not needed. On top of that, the claim was made that too many of BREL's workshops had been severely underutilised. Among its list of recommendations, the report suggested that the existing relationship between the BR board and BREL should cease, and that BREL should be broken up and privatised to encourage competition.[62]

The report was severely criticised by British Rail, the unions and other workers' representative bodies. The government made a show of rejecting the findings, but there can be little doubt that the recommendations in relation to BREL's monopoly of supplying and maintaining rolling stock for British Rail was already high on the agenda. This was a government that preached privatisation throughout every waking hour, and the Serpell Report had told it everything it wanted to hear.

Swindon's MP, David Stoddart, felt that if the proposals were implemented it would almost certainly lead to the closure of Swindon Works:

> This report will make Dr Beeching look like a saint. If the newspaper leaks are correct and the report is implemented by the Government it would be a hammer blow for Swindon. If there is any suggestion that the report is to be implemented in full or in part, we will oppose it very hard indeed!

Danny Lee, the Chairman of the Works Committee, was also quick to condemn the report:

> We will continue to fight the whole question of non-investment in railways. This would be total decimation of the railway system for purely ideological reasons. Beeching will pale into insignificance if what is rumoured comes about. It's crazy!

The comments in the local paper gave the indication that the report had been short-sighted, and should have focused on ways to equip the railways for the future, rather than cutting government support. The *Evening Advertiser* editorial stated that, 'Perhaps it is too much to hope for positive thinking in the present political climate.'[63]

Early in 1983, the BR Board's Director of Personnel, J. Palette, sent an official notification to all union representatives at the plants affected by BR's planned closures. Titled *BREL Capacity: The Plan for Closures,* Palette confirmed the timetable of run down and closure at the Temple Mills, Horwich and Shildon works, and went on to talk about the grim prospect for the future of BREL if things failed to improve: 'I think I must also caution that unless BREL succeeds in increasing its share of the world market for traction and rolling stock requirements, the probability of another medium-sized works closing within the 1986–87 timescale cannot be ruled out.'

This was taken as yet another warning shot that our jobs were still very much in the balance and all through 1983, with very small quantities of new work coming through the door, we wondered if or when that threat would be transformed into action.

On 22 March, the Shadow Secretary of State for Transport, Albert Booth, made his feelings known in the House of Commons in respect of what he said was a deliberate ploy to starve the British Rail workshops of work:

> The Government are running down British Rail by starving it of the investment needed for rolling stock, signalling and electrification. Therefore it is not surprising that British Rail orders for British Rail workshops have slumped. What is more serious for the workshops in general is the further run down that British Rail and British Rail Engineering Ltd are planning.

> It is the Government and not the British Railways Board who have set an investment ceiling, and then set an external financing limit that makes it impossible to attain that ceiling. By their commissioning of the Serpell Report and their attitude to the report, the Government have confirmed their anti-rail bias that has led us to this appalling decline in the prospects for British Rail.
>
> The spectre of unemployment now haunts the railway workshop towns.

The final coming together of workers from all of the affected sites occurred on 3 August 1983, when many hundreds of those employees under threat descended on London for a protest march in opposition to the damning implications of the Serpell Report. They first marched to a rally in Central Hall Westminster, before proceeding to the House of Commons.

Fifteen year-old Janette Purdham accompanied her father, Allen, on the journey from Shildon, and can be seen on the colour image of the Shildon contingent wearing a straw boater. 'I recall having a great day out. We met with the Deputy Leader of the Labour Party, Denis Healey; I vaguely remember him saying he admired my hat.'

On 3 August 1983 employees from all of the BREL workshops affected by job cuts demonstrated in London. (Tony Rima Collection)

That impressive and well-attended demonstration proved to be a rare moment of unity between the threatened workshops. A policy of non-collaboration between the representatives at the affected sites continued thereafter, right up until the closure of Shildon Works in July 1984. By May of that year it had become clear that the closures of Shildon, Horwich and Temple Mills were only stages in a much larger series of planned cuts and closures at BREL. By this time, Shildon openly refused to back campaigns at other plants, having felt that their own pleas for help had fallen on deaf ears. Shildon convenor John Priestley could not hide his frustration when speaking to a reporter form the local newspaper: 'I virtually went down on bended knees and pleaded for help from the other works last week – no other works has lifted a finger to help us.'[64]

There were marked differences between the strategies of the workers' representatives at the various sites as to how their members should approach the situation. For example, at Swindon the men who wanted to take voluntary redundancy were actively encouraged to do so, and they would often be assisted by their shop representative in an effort to secure the best redundancy package possible. This was in direct defiance of advice from union leaders, who had recommended that in the interest of solidarity the men should stay put. By the time of the August march, around 700 workers from Shildon had already taken voluntary redundancy, a decision that did not sit well with the works convenor, who 'toed the union line' by insisting that Shildon's best hope of survival would be for everyone to stick together. John Priestley went on the attack against those who had taken the money, stating that similar campaigns had failed for this very reason:

> There are some people going out I have no time for at all, and I wouldn't accept that they've done a good thing for Shildon at all. They've just cut and run; and they've cut and run to a situation that they have no job to go to at all. I'm sure within a couple of months they'll come running, asking for some support from us, and I don't think we'll be able to give it. They are frightened and confused.[65]

At Swindon, judging from the comments of Alun Rees above, the Works Committee took a different view, believing that if they cooperated with the management of BREL in its efforts to reorganise the works and to

August 1983: Demonstrators express their opposition to the Serpell Report. (Tony Rima Collection)

reduce the headcount without need for compulsory redundancies, then the management might take a more sympathetic view when the next round of cutbacks came along. The feeling was that if a man decided to go, then he would be safeguarding the future of a younger man.

As if we didn't already have enough to worry about on the shop floor at Swindon Works, things started to get even more worrying early in 1984 when I had begun to observe that many of the tracks upon which the coaches to be refurbished usually stood had gradually begun to look a lot more bare than they did previously, and stayed that way for much of the week. I certainly wasn't the only one to notice how sparse the workshop was beginning to look. Every time this happened a network of rumour spreading would almost immediately become activated. That most common of species in the rail works; the doom merchants, or prophets of doom as they were sometimes called, would suddenly find their voice. They would seize upon the slightest rumour and greatly exaggerate it for effect. I would often watch them huddling together in little groups, looking all around at the blank spaces on the internal tracks where they expected to see coaches being lined up for refurbishment; one by one they would slowly begin to shake their heads. Eventually they would arrive at the inevitable question that had been waiting patiently on the tips of their tongues throughout the entire 'performance': 'How many do you think will have to go this time?' This would trigger a round of wild speculation – figures ranging between a few hundred to more than 1,000 would be tossed into the mix, usually by those who felt comforted by their long service and believed themselves to be sure to avoid the next round of presumed job losses. You would never learn anything from the known doom merchants, and I soon learned to just ignore them, but you did reach a point where you just didn't know what or who to believe.

Things began to get more serious in early May 1984 when BREL management were due to meet behind closed doors to discuss the future of the various repair and refurbishment facilities, including Swindon. In anticipation of bad news, the unions threatened strike action in an attempt to put pressure on the management to spare the remaining 2,300 railway jobs they feared would be lost at Swindon Works. One top union official remarked, 'We have to toughen up or be crushed into the ground.' The contingent of around forty union men and Works Committee representatives who travelled to Euston on 1 May to lobby the meeting were startled to see a hearse draw up outside the main entrance containing a small group of men from Shildon Works, which by now was only weeks away from closure. Works convenor John Priestley again expressed his anger that more railway workers did not fight to save Shildon from the axe: 'The hearse has been brought here to take away Swindon Works. We warned people that unless they put up a fight, the works will be picked off one by one, and that's what's happening now.'[66]

The very next day, 2 May, a report of the meeting was leaked to the press indicating that the decision had been taken to close the Swindon Works. The local paper was published containing the banner headline 'Doomed – rail-works to close – 1,800 face the sack!' Even though the BREL management still refused to confirm the details of the leaked report, the figures spoke for themselves. BREL's Managing Director Philip Norman had informed an assembled press conference that at present there was only enough work in Swindon for 665 men if it survived until March 1987, indicating a required headcount reduction of 1,791. The employees' representatives stated loud and clear that they intended to fight any compulsory redundancies and to secure the future of the works. Many felt that they had been betrayed after reading the contents of the report, which stated that BREL Swindon was almost certain to close within three years. Also contained was an initial plan to slash the workforce by 700 immediately, hopefully through early retirement and voluntary redundancy. Civic leaders lamented that the heart would be ripped out of the town if this was allowed to happen, and the local press also reported the huge concerns of the local shopkeepers around the Rodbourne area who again feared for the future of their businesses.

The town's new Tory MP at the time, Simon Coombs, was vociferous in his condemnation of any impending decision to close Swindon, accusing the BREL management of, 'Frightening the Swindon workers to death every six months.' However, mere words were all he could offer and the unions made it clear they did not hold Mr Coombs in high regard after he had previously defended the Thatcher government's level of investment in Britain's railways. Even his attempts to find a buyer for the works from across the Atlantic received short shrift from the union men, who described the deal as a red herring and his words as hollow. Shop Steward Jim Devine made his feelings known to the local press: 'He [Simon Coombs] has got to understand that this is a fight against his Government. Last year he made similar noises then kicked us in the teeth by voting against us.'[67]

These were very worrying times for the workforce, most of whom had taken the leaked report at face value. They were further disheartened around the middle of May when the local council issued a report on the changing identity of Swindon. It was clear that manufacturing jobs had dropped significantly in the town, more than 11,000 jobs lost in the previous ten years to be precise. This equated to a quarter of the entire manufacturing labour force, a sector that previously made up 45 per cent of the total jobs in Swindon back in 1971. The spectacular increases of jobs in services and commerce – up 17,000 since 1971 – would be no consolation to the seemingly doomed rail workers, and neither would the 25 per cent increase in construction jobs during the same period. In the light of this report, the BREL bosses were urged by the local council to utilise the soon-to-be disused workshops in an effort help find or to create new jobs for the employees facing redundancy. One prominent member of the local clergy was imploring the Swindon railwaymen to pool all their redundancy money to help enable an ambitious buy-out scheme with the intention of keeping the works open.

The initial 700 redundancies, originally outlined in the leaked report of 2 May, were finally confirmed by the management, and although it was a shock when it finally came there was a feeling that the reduction in headcount could again be overcome without any need for compulsory redundancies. Many among the older employees who had hung on to their jobs during the earlier round of job cuts now opted for early redundancy once it had become all too obvious to them that the workshops no longer had a long-term future. Enhanced offers were made to coincide with the gradual drop off in workload as the carefully planned scale down gathered pace. More and more middle management staff also began to opt for the early redundancy option, or they would find additional employment more easily as their staff position effectively broadened their opportunities. This meant that workers were continually being 'made up' to fill the vacant positions. Men who had previously dressed in shabby overalls one day would suddenly appear clean-shaven and dressed in their best suit the next day. It got to the point where nobody knew what the management structure was, or who the top dog was any more. It was a bit like changing the captain of the *Titanic* an hour or so before the ship sank slowly into the murky depths of the Atlantic. It was particularly difficult for these men to carry out their duties at a time when nobody took them seriously, for even the established staff who hung on to the bitter end conceded that it was 'very difficult to maintain a professional attitude' under the circumstances.[68] There was a positive aspect to this middle management merry-go-round in that it did give the newly made up men an extra edge when it came to compiling their CVs when searching for a new beginning.

For the 2,000 or so of us that remained, the worry and speculation during those final months leading up to the eventual closure announcement seemed endless. Men would continue to scan the notice boards intensely, desperate for the news that they were all expecting, or in some cases even hoping for if only to get it over with. Now that the work seemed to be drying up all around us, it was as though everyone now knew for sure that their redundancy notice was getting very close. Men began to complain that they were being kept completely in the dark about their futures; 'We're like mushrooms,' they would forever complain, 'kept hidden in the dark and fed on ★★★★.' Committee men and union representatives never seemed to know anything, while middle management and most of the front-line bosses were totally unapproachable on the subject. I noticed that shop stewards had suddenly become less visible, and when you cornered one he always claimed to know no more than anybody else.

As the weeks rolled by, the local newspapers would crush your hopes in one article, while in another they would raise your spirits by seizing upon any words of optimism from higher up the ladder. The *Evening Advertiser* of 2 July 1984, asserted that, 'Swindon's railmen would be in line for a big hand-out after the local council had won Common Market cash for retraining the redundant employees.' Then barely three weeks later on 25 July, the same publication claimed that the 'Railworks had been let off the hook,' stating that, 'It would not close in 1986 (as many were predicting), but would remain in a vulnerable position.' Three days later, on 28 July, one left-wing councillor was branding the rail union chiefs as traitors for collaborating with BREL management to close down the Swindon Works. With so much contradictory reporting, you just never really knew where you stood.

Being an employees' representative at this time would no longer be just about resolving internal squabbles and carrying forward the grievances of individuals; suddenly there was a lot more at stake and things were about to get nasty. This was because during the initial stages of the run down, it wasn't so much the job cuts that mattered, for the first round of losses were absorbed by early retirement and voluntary redundancy. What mattered then was the increasing amount of redeployment throughout the works, the process that would be required to keep people in jobs. Redeployment and retraining became the buzz words as the management sought to fit so many square pegs into round holes in an effort to keep the inactive percentage of the workforce busy. This was nothing new as there were many men who had been retrained or redeployed when the headcount had previously been reduced in the 1960s and '70s. Some trades had disappeared altogether, with the surplus men having been amalgamated into the closest relating trade – the most typical example was when polishers were required to become painters. This time around, a new initiative known as 'dual skills' was launched, with the idea being that employees could be provided with additional skills, enabling them to be more easily moved to areas where a shortage of labour had occurred. Ted Jefferies was instrumental in putting this initiative into motion, as his son Mark remembers:

It took a long time to train people, and there was a fair bit of union resistance. But in time, fitters and turners became upholsterers; upholsterers became electricians or coppersmiths and so on … As time went on more people became dual-skilled and it began to show on the balance sheet. Gradually the figures went from showing a catastrophic loss to a balanced account, and then into the final two years, a healthy profit. I remember dad's disbelief that Swindon Works was being closed whilst in profit, when Eastleigh Works continued to show massive losses. Dad concluded that the land that the works sat on was worth considerably more than the profit being made.

Mark Jefferies

There are differing recollections from the former railmen who were required to learn dual skills. Lorne McCalla, who was required to retrain as an electrician, remembers there was 'zero exposure to proper training', and that the 'dual skills people' were unpopular with the established electricians, who were anxious to protect their own jobs'. Stephen Warner also discovered a measure of resentment when he was required to be retrained: 'I finished my vehicle builder apprenticeship at age 20, then had to be retrained as a boilermaker. It wasn't a happy sector to work in, as I think they resented us trainees and never missed a chance to stitch you up.'

Chris Rees was in the first batch to be 'retrained' from vehicle builder to fitter, an opportunity that ultimately helped him relocate to the Plymouth depot, where he still works 'off the tools' today. Overall, the dual-skills project had proved to be a successful initiative, and the additional skills and experience was a potentially useful acquisition for those employees. However, with every passing month the numbers of trades that were being reduced in numbers or dispensed with altogether was increasing. A particularly large gang of surplus employees (referred to as the A Team) was formed to perform maintenance tasks around the workshops. With increasing regularity the shop stewards were required to inform a fully indentured tradesman that he would now have to take a semi or unskilled job, and to report to a distant work station such as the Spring Shop, the asbestos house or the foundry, or to some other working environment he wasn't used to. It was a stark choice – you either took the redundancy money, or you took the job being offered if you wanted to remain in employment. It was as though those once highly valued skills possessed by generations of time-served men were no longer required, as the demands made upon their abilities gradually diminished during those final years of run down and closure. Vehicle builder Andy Witcher's account typifies what went on at the works around this time: 'I was told there were no longer any jobs on my section and was offered a position as a Category 2 Painter washing windows. Definitely not my thing, so I left after about a month. Still, I always look back on my time in the railway works as being great times.'

Jim Bateman became one of the last British Rail-employed apprentices to come out of his time, and was to be redeployed on three occasions when the work for the No. 19 Shop vehicle builders began to dry up:

> After just six months working in my chosen profession in 19 shop, I went into work one morning only to be handed a broom by a supervisor (affectionately known as Ayatollah) and being told, 'This will be your job from now on.' So here I was, on the wages of a craftsman sweeping the floor. After that they gave me the job of maintaining the coolant levels on all the centre lathes. Finally, I got transferred to a small team charged with stripping out the copper piping from the condemned locos. This involved spending a few months standing in puddles of diesel and retrieving what copper we could. There was lots of funny banter between the guys, which made the job bearable. I didn't stick around to get my redundancy. I considered a steady job offer to be more important and left as soon as an opportunity arose.

As far as us painters were concerned, we soon realised we would have to fight our own battles. This would mean having to approach the management directly if we were to avoid being stitched up during this process. The ever-dwindling lack of any available or effective direct representation, particularly towards the end, merely added to our cynicism of the way we felt things were being conducted. We kept receiving sealed instructions detailing us where to report the next day, without any effective support or advice – what had been the point of those nine years of union subs? More than once I'd heard a shop steward advising young lads to 'take the money' rather than take the fight to the management to have the lad 'kept on' – at least to give him an opportunity to find another job before being flung out onto the streets. Because of this, it became a purple patch for black humour among the men. For example, it became a standing joke that we would finally learn about our redundancies from the pages of the local evening paper, rather than from our employers or our representatives. Even when the workshops were half bare, and it seemed obvious to everyone that the Swindon Works was effectively finished, we were still being told absolutely nothing. A lot of the fight had gone from the workforce by August 1984 when union leaders arranged a mass rally in Farringdon Road Park, with Labour's transport spokesman John Prescott among those lined up to address the workforce. Works Committee Vice-Chairman Graham Humphries called for 100 per cent support, indicating that 'it was essential to keep the centre of attention focused on the rail works'. As things turned out, only 150 rail workers out of the remaining 2,000 workforce bothered to brave the rain and listen to the speakers, some of whom expressed dismay that the employees 'would rather go home, than try to save their jobs'.[69]

On 4 August 1984 there was a disappointingly low turnout in Farringdon Road Park to hear Labour's transport spokesman John Prescott speak in support of the threatened rail workers. (Andy Binks, The Swindon Society)

A few days later, on 10 August, Swindon workers were urged to attend a huge march and demonstration against workshop closures in Derby, involving up to 5,000 employees from all BREL workshops, with the intention being to cripple production for the day nationwide. The workers who would not be attending were asked to stop work at lunchtime – effectively to stage a half-day strike. The planned demonstration descended into farce when the specially chartered train to take 400 demonstrators from Swindon to Derby was cancelled owing to industrial action on the part of other NUR members who had walked out in sympathy. Thereafter, the Swindon contingent had nowhere to go, other than to hang around Swindon station. The only emergency conference held that day was on the fate of the 600 sandwiches packed for the journey. They were eventually handed out to commuters.[70] Works Committee Chairman Danny Lee accused BR of sabotaging the demonstration, claiming that they had known the train would be sidelined eight hours before they informed him – leaving him no time to make alternative arrangements.

Back in Swindon, we had all followed the fortunes of the other BR engineering works on the notice boards. First it had been Ashford in Kent, soon followed by Temple Mills, then Horwich, and now Shildon was in its final death rattle. The workshops were indeed being picked off one by one as Shildon convenor John Priestley had suggested. Just about every railway employee in Swindon felt they already knew which works would be next. Similarly, everyone knew that British Rail's top brass would look after the workshops to whom they possessed a particular affiliation. 'The Management Committee are a lot closer to Derby and Crewe than they are to Swindon,' you would hear men say. This was typical of the cynicism that prevailed as railway employees in workshops across the country braced themselves in anticipation of the next wielding of the axe by BREL's board of directors.

As bleak at things looked in the mid-1980s, one had to feel sorry for those final apprentices that had been admitted into the works, having come across from the Works Training School in 1983. These lads still required another two to three years more training to be able to finish their apprenticeships, and were at least given some assistance in finding alternative companies to sponsor them through to the end of their time. Others from the previous year barely had any time to take up their trades before they were being offered a stark choice between being redeployed into a menial or labour-intensive, low-skilled position, or to take voluntary redundancy. Many took the money and wound up doing something totally different from what they had been trained to do for the past three or four years. It seemed like such a waste of precious time – especially for those who were in very railway-specific trades. By this time, the ambition and enthusiasm that the Works Training School staff had instilled within those lads during the first highly enjoyable twelve months now seemed a very distant memory. Kevin Weaver oversaw many of the remaining apprentices through those final years, and praised them for their attitude:

> They just had to keep going; they had to switch off from what was going on around them and focus on completing the required tasks and keeping their log books up to date. Without that official account of their training schedule, including having all the required specifications ticked off as completed, they could not finish their apprenticeships.

8

THE AXE FALLS

By the middle of 1984 the all too obvious running-down process was starting to take effect; it was becoming increasingly more difficult to look busy when the big wigs were about. Because of this I had seized an opportunity to transfer to the night shift. 'Out of sight, out of mind,' I thought, and then when the workload dropped off even further there was barely enough work coming through the doors to keep men on their toes for half of the nine-and-a-half-hour shift. This was a situation that made for what seemed like a much longer night spent mostly watching the clock ticking off the hours. We all felt totally demoralised by this state of affairs. The management had attempted to pick everybody up in a letter inserted into their pay packets at the end of November, claiming that the works would enjoy a full-capacity workload for the next eighteen months. As much as we wanted to believe it, there was little evidence of a full-capacity workload on the night shift in 19A Shop.[71]

Prior to the drop off in workload, the general rule on nights in the Paint Shop had always been to get through your allocation of work as quickly as possible, leaving you plenty of time to take things a bit easier at the back end of the shift when the fatigue began to bite. Now with barely half a night's work for the gang, one got to the point where you would find a suitable carriage for the purpose of having a doze, preferably one with comfortable seats inside that were not too dirty. Some men would just prefer to soldier on, painting door edges again, or looking for jobs to do just to make the shift go a bit quicker. Others would 'sit it out' playing cards or reading until dawn. One of the guys would always walk around waking anybody up who

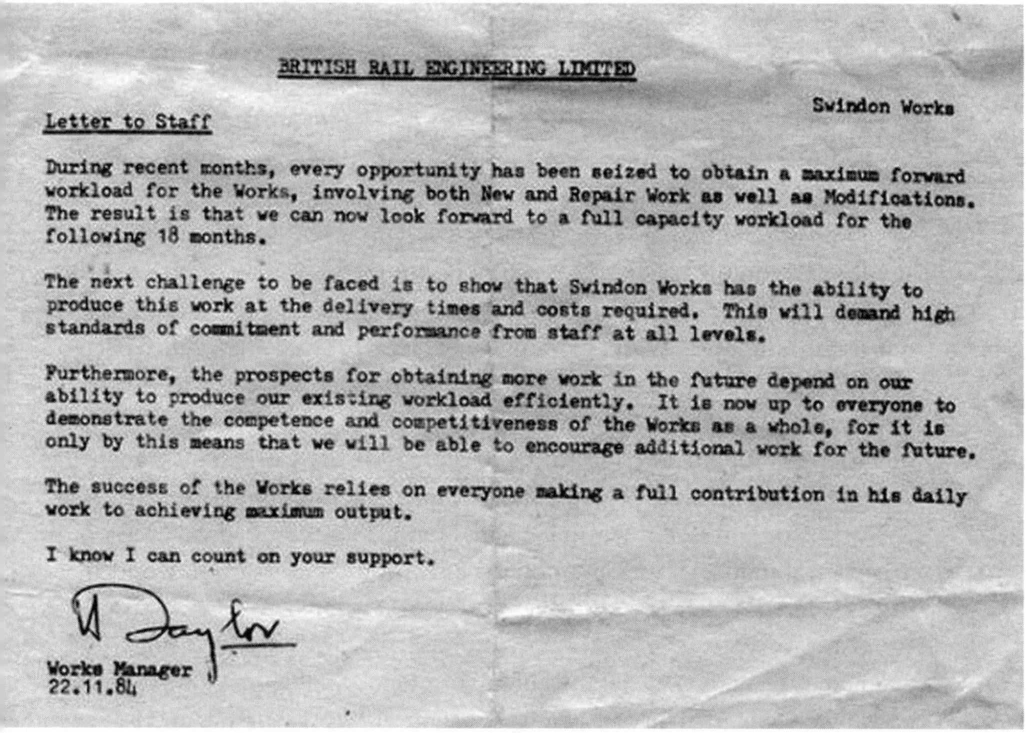

BRITISH RAIL ENGINEERING LIMITED

Swindon Works

Letter to Staff

During recent months, every opportunity has been seized to obtain a maximum forward workload for the Works, involving both New and Repair Work as well as Modifications. The result is that we can now look forward to a full capacity workload for the following 18 months.

The next challenge to be faced is to show that Swindon Works has the ability to produce this work at the delivery times and costs required. This will demand high standards of commitment and performance from staff at all levels.

Furthermore, the prospects for obtaining more work in the future depend on our ability to produce our existing workload efficiently. It is now up to everyone to demonstrate the competence and competitiveness of the Works as a whole, for it is only by this means that we will be able to encourage additional work for the future.

The success of the Works relies on everyone making a full contribution in his daily work to achieving maximum output.

I know I can count on your support.

Works Manager
22.11.84

In November 1984 all Swindon rail workers received a letter from the Works Manager in their wage packets guaranteeing them eighteen months' work – most of them went 'down the slope' long before that time period had elapsed.

happened to be dozing before the first of the day shift guys began to arrive. There was never any danger of you getting caught out if you happened to fall asleep, for only one foreman staffed the whole factory during the night time in those final years, and he didn't much care what you got up to so long as you got all of your allocated work done. By the time that such practices as grabbing an hour's kip began to occur, we were already defeated men who knew that our days were numbered. During the daytime many of the men were already engaged in trying to start businesses of their own in readiness for the calamity that would soon befall them, and the chance of getting a couple of hours' kip in an almost desolate workshop was too good an opportunity to pass up.

Having said that, it was also evident that even at this late stage a lot of the men still had their pride and still seized any opportunity to do a good job, even though they realised that the writing was on the wall.

Eventually that long-dreaded day finally arrived and on 16 May 1985 we finally learned that Swindon Works was to close down completely before the end of March 1986. The main headline in the local paper that day read 'The End of the Line', after the final execution of the works was announced at talks with union leaders at a meeting in Luton. After years of doubt and uncertainty, it was clear that this time there would be no reprieve for the remaining employees. Works Committee Secretary Terry Larkham had been among those leading the fight to save the works and was quick to express his anger at the decision: 'It is an absolute betrayal. A stab in the back after all our cooperation and our agreement to reorganise the works. The workers should make themselves a bloody nuisance now that there is nothing to lose!'

Works Committee Chairman Graham Humphries described the decision as 'an act of industrial vandalism on a massive scale' and was highly critical of government policy:

> There is enough work on the railway to produce rolling stock to keep Swindon going, but they are putting out contracts to Sweden and America. We have a government hell-bent on privatising everything that moves, selling off the assets and ignoring the four million unemployed.

The leader of Thamesdown Council, Arthur Miles, also expressed his shock and anger at the decision in the *Swindon Evening Advertiser* that day: 'This is a bombshell. This is a disaster. This is much more serious than we feared. We were given assurances that about 700 would be kept in work.'

Swindon councillors were also quick to condemn the government, claiming the decision to close the works had been political, having deliberately starved the industry of cash during the years leading up to the announcement. Other local dignitaries also voiced their concerns through the local press. The town's MP said he was 'Sad, but not surprised' by the decision, and said he intended to press for an emergency commons debate on the issue. Union leaders were much more scathing in their condemnation of the decision and turned their anger on the Thatcher government's policies: 'The Iron Lady has smashed 150 years of hard work,' stormed NUR shop steward Bob Kennedy.[72]

Right: Original programme cover for the naming ceremony of *Evening Star* on 18 March 1960. (Swindon Advertiser Archive)

Below: Centre section of the programme published ahead of the naming ceremony for *Evening Star*. The images beneath *Evening Star* show the *Premier* on the left, the first Swindon-built freight locomotive completed in February 1846, and, on the right, the first Swindon-built passenger locomotive the *Great Western*, completed in April of the same year. (*Swindon Advertiser* Archive)

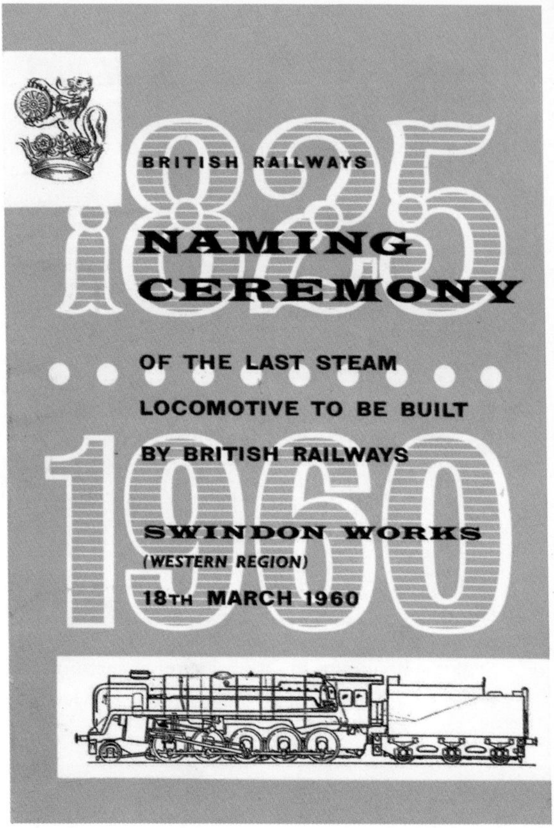

Class 9F 2–10–0 locomotive No. 92220
Built at Swindon March, 1960.

" Premier " The first freight engine built at Swindon. February, 1846.

" Great Western " The first passenger engine built at Swindon. April, 1846.

Staff assembling for the special naming ceremony for the final steam locomotive built for British Railways, *Evening Star*, Swindon Works, 18 March 1960. (J.A. Coiley, National Railway Museum)

City of Truro entering the GWR Railway Museum in 1961, where it remained until 1985. Now a permanent exhibit in STEAM: Museum of the Great Western Railway. (T.B. Owen, Colour rail)

Class 42 Warships under construction at Swindon Works in 1960. (T.B. Owen, Colour rail)

The Works Training School represented a fresh approach to pre-apprenticeship training by aiming to place the trainee into the trade for which he was best suited. (Roy Hazell Collection)

Above: Ron Williams and Ron Bizley painting the black chevrons on a shunter locomotive. (Pete Gradidge)

Opposite above: The diesel testing bays in No. 19 Shop. I often had to sign-write these vehicles, accompanied by the loud noise of the engines running flat out. (Keith Miller)

Opposite below: Payday! The famous black pay tables were always assembled with military precision and the paying out process executed with maximum efficiency! (Tony Rima Collection)

King George V boiler arriving at Swindon Works' A Shop for inspection and repair. (Tony Rima Collection)

Opposite above: King George V boiler on the stand prior to repair. (Tony Rima Collection)

Opposite below: No. 19A Shop. The award of a sizable contract in 1979 to overhaul the Southern EMU fleet led to the recruitment of 1,000 extra workers. (Tony Rima Collection)

7188

Gatherings of large numbers on the traverser table prior to paying out was usually where the latest rumours were swapped between sections. (Tony Rima Collection)

Swindon MP David Stoddart addressing the workforce in Farringdon Road Park in May 1982. (Tony Rima Collection)

On 7 May 1982 the biggest demonstrations Swindon has ever seen took place when around 3,000 railway workers marched through the streets in protest against BREL's planned 1,516 job cuts at the works. (Tony Rima Collection)

Above: On 3 August 1983, Swindon's rail-men joined other BREL workers from all the remaining workshops in a march on Westminster to lobby MPs in protest against planned job cuts and workshop closures. (Tony Rima Collection)

Opposite above: Threatened BREL employees from across the country streaming across Waterloo Bridge in August 1983. (Tony Rima Collection)

Opposite below: On 3 August 1983 employees from the doomed Shildon Works demonstrate in London. Fifteen-year-old Janette Purdham (second from the left, wearing a hat) can be seen in front of her father, Allen. (Tony Rima Collection)

FALSE PROMISES FROM B.R.E.L.
NO JOB CUTS AT SHILDON
OUR PROUD RECORD MUST NOT DIE
SHILDON CAN WIN WITH A LITTLE HELP FROM IT'S FRIENDS.
THE REWARD FOR EFFICIENCY
SHILDON

On 29 May 1985 around 350 Swindon rail-men arrived in London to demonstrate at a British Rail management meeting before marching on to Westminster to lobby MPs. (Tony Rima Collection)

Left: Fitters Alan Selwood and Wilf Dawson about to lift the final overhauled English Electric 6KT power unit from its stand in March 1986. (Chris Rees)

Below: Black Wednesday, 26 March 1986, and workers are being paid out on the final day. One rail-man emerges from the office holding his redundancy package aloft. (Tony Rima Collection)

Redundant rail workers leaving for the final time through the West Gate in Rodbourne Road on Black Wednesday. The local press are in attendance. (Chris Rees)

Left: Black Wednesday – the final moments before everyone walked out leaving everything the way it was, right down to the 'Page 3 girls' on the walls. (Andy Binks, The Swindon Society)

Below: The famous works' hooter gives off one final long blast on Black Wednesday. (Andy Binks, The Swindon Society)

Above: July 1986, the last remaining BREL Swindon office staff. Back row: Ruth Butcher, Tom Foulds, Jack Miles, Ken Tanner, Dave Ellis, Kevin Weaver. Font row: Anita Hughes, Julia Bond, Sheila Short, Janet Cook, Lesley Goldby, Stuart Wakeley, Elaine Hulford, Dave Sheppard. (Kevin Weaver)

Left: Tearing down the huge A Shop. (Brian Robert Marshall)

The demolition of A Shop. One of its many cranes lies twisted and broken prior to being cut up for scrap. (Brian Robert Marshall)

The mighty A Shop prior to demolition (above) and the site cleared (below). (Jason McCormick/ Neil Lover, Swindon's Other Railway)

National Railway Museum on Tour: Swindon 1990. *Evening Star* on display in No. 19 Shop alongside its replacement, the Class 52 D1000 *Western*. (Paul Gulliver)

The run down towards closure was to begin on 1 September of that year with the final closure planned for the end of March seven months later. A total of 1,200 BREL jobs would also be lost at Glasgow, 400 at Eastleigh and 350 at Doncaster. Smaller numbers of redundancies were announced for other works, bringing the total of railway engineering job losses announced that day to 4,800. It was estimated that the male jobless figure for Swindon would rise by 35 per cent as a result of the decision made that day, the figure being boosted by additional jobs lost in other businesses linked to the Swindon Works.[73]

Even though we'd known it was coming for years, it still felt like a devastating blow when you finally saw it in black and white. Those prophets of doom who had for many years been churning out the same tired old rhetoric that nothing would ever save us from 'going down the slope' were finally having their day. After several minutes of vitriolic condemnation of a government that could allow this to happen, those same employees were soon busy calculating the expected value of their redundancy pay-outs. These discussions quickly erupted into disagreements regarding to what they thought they would be entitled. Other employees could not contain their anger. It was reported that around 400 furious workers had downed tools shortly after the announcement and marched to the Swindon Works main building to vent their anger at the management. Chants of anti-British Rail rhetoric filled the air, and one man waved a hangman's noose at personnel director Alan Dunkley when he returned back from the damning meeting in Luton. His pleas in the face of their direct anger for the men to calm down and be sensible fell on deaf ears. Former Works Manager Harry Roberts admitted he was dumbfounded that the axe had finally fallen on Swindon, having previously worked so hard to stave off closure a decade earlier. Roberts was particularly scathing in his criticism of the Thatcher government, and spoke to reporters from the *Evening Advertiser* on the day the closure was announced: 'I'm shattered by the news, my head is still reeling. The works has fallen victim to a government of asset strippers and property speculators who want to turn it over as a prime site for developers.'

It was the job of Parliamentary Under-Secretary of State for the Department of Transport David Mitchell MP to impart the news of the BREL board's decision to the House of Commons that afternoon:

> At a meeting of its joint consultative committee on 15 May, the management of British Rail Engineering Ltd. informed the unions that it had reluctantly come to the conclusion that it would be necessary to make further reductions in manpower within BREL. A year ago, the management had already informed the unions at the equivalent meeting of proposed reductions. Its latest evaluation of work load, however, shows a further reduction of 13 per cent in repair work. The company has therefore concluded that it needs to reduce manpower by a further 1,300 over the next two years.
>
> The demand for railway repair and maintenance has declined because of British Rail's decision to invest in new rolling stock. In particular, investment in new diesel multiple units with higher performance means that the same frequency of service can now be provided with fewer trains, and each of these fewer units requires less maintenance. Major programmes of refurbishment, particularly the stripping of asbestos from older vehicles, are also nearing completion, and this has been a significant part of the recent workload.
>
> In the light of this reduced demand, British Rail and BREL have, with considerable regret, decided that they must propose to the unions a sizeable rundown of the Glasgow Springburn works and some further manpower reductions at other works, particularly Doncaster and Eastleigh. Most regrettably of all, they have decided, after considering the position carefully, that there is insufficient work to maintain the BREL works at Swindon after March 1986.
>
> I know that these proposals will be a hard blow to the communities concerned, particularly to Swindon, but British Rail and BREL have considered the matter carefully and concluded that a reduction of capacity of this scale is unavoidable. There will, of course, be an opportunity for all the possibilities to be re-examined fully in the consultations with the employees which now follow BREL's announcement.
>
> British Rail and BREL will do all that they can to find alternative work for redundant employees by offering opportunities to transfer to other works and by encouraging business development and job creation at both Swindon and Glasgow.[74]

Swindon's MP Simon Coombs rose quickly to his feet, demanding that British Rail be pressed to seek redeployment for as many of the soon-to-be redundant workforce as could be achieved. Labour MP Dennis Skinner chipped in that the honourable gentleman would soon be redeployed, a comment that elicited howls of laughter from the chamber. But this was clearly no laughing matter. The knock-on effect of this decision would also impact on dozens of other Swindon firms that supplied such things as timber, metal, oil and office equipment, not to mention the road hauliers who delivered the equipment. The *Evening Advertiser* reported on 23 May that 'hundreds of jobs could be lost in other firms if the rail works shuts'. Mr Coombs then went on to demand that, 'Swindon rail workers be given redundancy payments by British Rail on the same level as those granted this year to people in other nationalised industries.' Shadow Transport Minister Gwyneth Dunwoody accused BR Chairman Bob Reid of, 'Cutting his own throat by spending abroad, rather than expanding BREL – a strategy that would cost the Government £29 million in unemployment cheques and lost taxes, not to mention the fortune it would cost BR in redundancy payments.'

By the time everyone returned to work the following morning on 17 May, the fight to save the works was gathering at a pace. A Swindon Railworks Defence Committee had been formed that would operate alongside the Joint Works Committee in taking the fight as far as they possibly could. Union leaders were already predicting that a national rail strike would take place in support of the Swindon workers.

The official line from BREL was relayed time and again whenever the Swindon workers representatives and members of the BREL Board of Directors came together for further discussion. The axe had fallen on Swindon, because in the eyes of the BREL Board of Directors, it was exclusively a repair and refurbishment facility. The maintenance and repair of existing rolling stock was being cut by around 13 per cent, and Swindon would have to absorb the greater part of this major contraction in the projected workload. This amounted to 1,600 job cuts that would have to be spread throughout those locations dedicated to repair and refurbishment work, which at the time amounted to 83 per cent of the entire BREL workload. It was impressed upon the Works Committee representatives that within four years, owing to the ageing rolling stock, only 40 per cent of future rail-engineering contracts would be classified as repair work, alongside 60 per cent being new-build. In short, huge investment had been earmarked for new rolling stock, meaning there would be much less maintenance required.

Thereafter, the Works Committee members took every opportunity to hammer the Thatcher government over its deliberate lack of investment in British industry. At the annual TASS Conference in Bournemouth, Committee Secretary Graham Humphries accused the government of 'doing more damage to UK industry than the German High Command during the last war!'

Within days of the decision to close Swindon Works, Works Manager Harold Taylor was being accused by shop stewards of deliberately sabotaging the fight against closure by preventing meetings from taking place. Works Committee Chairman Terry Larkham expressed his anger over 'glossy videos' being sent out to staff at other works explaining why Swindon had to close: 'They [BREL] are putting out mountains of propaganda to try and isolate us from our colleagues in the rest of the country. They didn't even have the decency to show us copies of what was going around.'

BREL's response was that they didn't send them to Swindon as they didn't want to be seen as 'rubbing their noses in it'. This management interference did not stop the various committees from coordinating a plan of action. The workers' representatives vowed again that it would be a 'fight to the death'. Terry Larkham said, 'The blokes are very, very angry. We have already got the full support from the council and the public of this town. Basically, the workers here are going to make a bloody nuisance of themselves – we are not going away.'

This anger had been further exacerbated by the decision of Works Committee Chairman Danny Lee to abandon the fight in order to take up a management role with the Swindon Holdings company set up by BR to create jobs for redundant railmen. Workers felt as though their leader had known all along what was coming and then jumped into bed with the opposition in an act of self-preservation. Theories about the inevitability of what had happened were widespread throughout the works. Trimming Shop foreman Stan Scott believed the closure date to have been predestined in the sense that March 1986 had been the date earmarked for closure many years previously:

> I was an apprentice in 1964 and was made redundant in 1970. When I returned in January 1976 we had so much work like you wouldn't believe. It was Harry Roberts, the then Works Manager, who breathed new life

> into the works for those last ten years. I remember saying to George Scotford, a union executive, 'This will do me until I retire,' and he replied, 'You will be out of here by March 1986 and this site will be sold off.' I didn't believe him, but it appears he was right. Ten years work we were told and ten years we got.
>
> Stan Scott, Trimming Shop foreman

The first move from the joint committees had been to call a one-day strike for 29 May and to boycott all of the GWR anniversary celebrations; both proposals were carried unanimously by the members. Swindon had been due to play a central role in these celebrations, and although preparations had gone ahead, plans for a special exhibition were eventually cancelled. On top of this the members agreed to an indefinite overtime ban and reaffirmed their complete refusal to cooperate with any reorganisation in the works. A large number of employees, accompanied by their union representatives, would march on Westminster to lobby MPs, also on 29 May, for support in helping to fight the case for saving the works. A few days earlier, on 25 May, a petition was launched by the Transport Salaried Staff Association with the ambitious target of one million signatures. A couple of days after that it would be the wives and girlfriends who came out fighting with the announcement that a Women's Support Group was being formed.

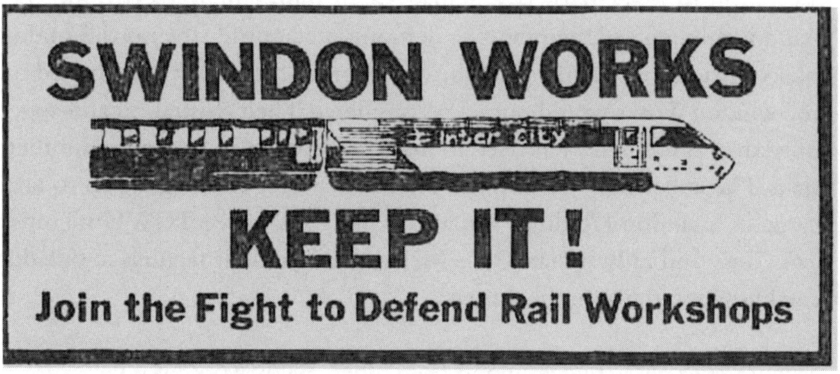

Stickers such as this appeared all across the town following the closure announcement. (Roy Hazell Collection)

At a special meeting of Thamesdown Borough Council that evening the Labour-run council also voted to boycott the GWR 150th Anniversary celebrations. Aside from Swindon Works' original plan to host a spectacular display of steam locomotives and railway memorabilia, there had also been plans for a huge trade exhibition to be held at a site nearby and a children's fête in Farringdon Rd Park. The council effectively binned the whole project, and instead promised cash aid for the soon-to-be redundant workforce. The only 'event' in Swindon to mark the 150th Anniversary was a special edition of *Songs of Praise* that the BBC had already recorded. On 20 May, at least three Labour councillors including Eamonn Hackett made their feelings known to the *Swindon Evening Advertiser*: 'How can you celebrate something when you know you have families with children who are going to be on the dole? It's absolutely disgusting!'

Councillor Rosemary Clifford felt that the men had a right to their jobs, and must be defended by the council and the town, while councillor Malcolm Sargeant thought the effects on the town would be 'potentially devastating'.

There was very little unity between Labour and Tory councillors at the meeting when the ruling Labour group refused to remove a clause laying the blame firmly at the Tory government's door due to its deliberate lack of investment. This led to Tory councillors abstaining from the motion. A few days later the council announced that it was also pulling out of the Swindon Holdings Company that had been set up by British Rail in an effort to create jobs.

Come 29 May, the day of the strike, union leaders and employees travelled to London to meet with BR management representatives. Around 350 Swindon railmen and their families demonstrated outside the north London hotel, only to be told firmly that the death sentence that had been passed on the Swindon Works would not be reconsidered. Their frustration and anger boiled over as union leaders tried to make speeches in an attempt to lift their spirits. The anger they felt towards Danny Lee over his resignation to take charge of Swindon Holdings was also plain for all to see. TGWU member Alan Close and railwayman Dave McVeigh made their feelings about this issue known to the assembled press:

> How are we going to get support from other railway workshops when we agreed under Mr Lee's leadership to let Shildon and Horwich shut down. All along we toed the bosses' line.

Above left: May 1985. Workers gather at Paddington Station prior to marching on Westminster. (Tony Rima Collection)

Above right: Paddington Station – the fight to save Swindon Works, 29 May 1985. (Tony Rima Collection)

> We haven't got much chance now. We have been well and truly stitched up. We followed Danny Lee like lambs to the slaughter.

Shop stewards had previously expressed disbelief at a statement from Mr Lee expressing his anger at the announcement. He claimed he did not know about the decision to close the works and that he had acted in good faith when he took up the management position. As far as Works Committee man and NUR member Harold Sealey was concerned, Lee was now history, and the fight to save the works from closure had to go on:

> I will be asking my union for total support – no longer are the Swindon blokes going to be left in the dark. If at the end of the day it means we have to use our industrial muscle then we will. I have been in the trade union movement for thirty-seven years and I'm not selling my job now!

Meanwhile, back at the works, the twenty-four-hour strike in protest at the closure plans had been a huge success, with only a handful of the remaining

With just days to go before the closure, workers scan the noticeboards for possible job or retraining opportunities. (*Swindon Advertiser*)

2,300 workers crossing the picket line. Shop steward Jim Devine told the *Swindon Evening Advertiser* that day that British Rail would have a fight on their hands if they didn't back down: 'Everyone thought Swindon would lie down and die – but the response today shows that this isn't going to happen. The full anger of our lads is going to be vented outside these talks – and British Rail had better take notice!'

From that month onwards, every related item of news published in the local paper was positioned beneath the common heading 'Death of the Railworks'. This, along with the continued pessimism of those last remaining merchants of doom, merely helped to foster a feeling of resignation throughout the workforce. As valiant as our representatives tried, we all knew deep down very soon that it was probably futile, and that from that day forward we would have to start thinking seriously about our futures.

The BREL management organised the first of many advice seminars for groups of workers offering guidance on how best to adapt to the situation, along with advice on various job-search methods and so forth. The seminars usually incorporated around two dozen employees at a time, and there was never any one-to-one counselling. I was still working night shift at the time, which meant that my night-shift colleagues and I felt isolated to a degree from any of the support initiatives on offer. I was very much in a similar position to the one I had been in when I left school a decade earlier. I was heading towards Black Wednesday with no clear idea of what I was going to do. It was a situation in which the number of people applying for skilled manual positions would be counted in their hundreds. One thing I did know for certain was that I didn't want to carry on painting for the remainder of my working life and I began to look ever more closely at the retraining packages on offer courtesy of the Manpower Services Commission.

9

THE LAST DAYS AND BLACK WEDNESDAY

It is often said that tradition dies hard. This was particularly so back in those final few weeks at the Swindon Works when the day we would finally go down that much-maligned slope drew ever closer. Those final days of clocking on for the night shift, a very long night with little or no available work left for us to do, only served to further compound our bitterness. The absolute silence inside those vast, dimly lit workshops in the dead of night is something I will never forget. I said earlier that I didn't believe in ghosts, but I knew only too well that at that moment those dark and desolate buildings were full of them. Almost a century and a half of glorious history was now reduced to silent darkness, save for the distant hum of an overlooked ventilation unit or the hiss of a leaking hot water pipe.

The battle to save Swindon Works had all but ended by the time we returned to the works after the Christmas break of 1985. The Swindon Works Committee and the Swindon Railway Works Defence Committee had taken the fight as far as they could, all the way to No. 10 Downing Street. One workers representative even went so far as to lay down on the track in protest when the newly repaired 'pride of Swindon', the *King George V*, was about to be demonstrated before an invited gathering of dignitaries. Despite all the talk of past glories, the endless fighting talk, the protest march for jobs and the lobbying at Westminster, the fight to save the works from closure had all been to no avail. The comment column by Lynn Barlow in the *Swindon Evening Advertiser* on Black Wednesday offered an accurate summary of the way things were:

> Graffiti chalked on lockers and walls is virtually all that's left of the anger. Emotional messages from rail workers who now stand in small groups chatting. That's about all they do now. What would once have been a barely discernible hammer tap echoes round the principle [*sic*] workshop. For now in A Shop, machinery lies idle.

Those employee representatives hell-bent on fighting against the closure to the last were never going to get much joy out of the government of the day. In one last act of desperation, a petition containing more than 25,000 signatures was presented to the Transport Secretary Nicholas Ridley on 21 March, just five days before the date set for closure. The fate of the works did find sympathy in some unlikely places. On the green lawns of Buckingham Palace during one of her many garden parties, Her Majesty the Queen felt sufficiently moved to express feelings of sadness upon hearing news of the impending closure of Swindon's famous old Great Western Railway Works.[75] The young Princess Elizabeth had been an enthusiastic visitor to the works back in November 1950 for the official naming of the Star-class locomotive *The Princess Elizabeth*, after which she had also been presented with a small model of the locomotive bearing her title.[76] Now, thirty-five years later, she informed Mayor of Thamesdown Harry Garrett, 'That it was very sad that it looked likely they were going to close.'

One week before the closure, a special service was held at St Mary's as 'A thanksgiving for the effort of generations of railway workers'. The town's industrial chaplain, the Rev. Graham Potter, read out a sombre message of hope for the redundant railwaymen: 'There may be tears. There may be sadness. But let there be real hope that together we can build a future.'

The repercussions had also begun in earnest with the expected blame game being slugged out in the local press. The chief target was the town's MP Simon Coombes, who was accused by union leaders of not having done enough to try and save the works. One union leader reminded the local electorate that, 'They need to remember that at the ballot box.' Mr Coombs furiously denied that he hadn't done enough, insisting that, despite having voted with the government against a Labour motion that might have improved the Swindon Works' chances of survival, he had simply tried and failed in his efforts to get the BR board to reconsider.[77] Former Works Manager Harry Roberts, whose efforts had previously extended the life of the facility, expressed his determination to help in some way towards improving the opportunities for

Graffiti scrawled on lockers was all that remained of the fight to save the works. (*Swindon Advertiser*)

the redundant rail workers. A new consortium known as Great Western Works Ltd had recently joined the running to take over the 150-acre site, and Mr Roberts had agreed to take on the role of production engineering consultant. Regrettably the project never succeeded in taking over control of the location.

During those final weeks, what remained of the Swindon management team engaged the Manpower Services Commission and the Swindon Enterprise Council in an effort to provide some continued measure of support and advice for the men, some of whom had no clue regarding what they would do when the end finally came. By the time the closure was announced most of the older GWR hands had departed, meaning the majority of those who remained were still very much of working age. A large number of those remaining had been employed in 1979 on the back of the Southern Region EMU order; many among them were not what you would call dyed-in-the-wood railmen; they had seen it all before and were more confident of getting fixed up with something. For those skilled in railway-specific trades, those various retraining schemes administered by the MSC would prove to be a popular option, with most of the classes being filled to capacity. The Swindon Enterprise Council also began presenting seminars on the subject of a business start-up scheme, complete with an offer of a £1,000 grant to help you on your way if certain criteria were met (and they were stiff criteria, believe me!). The 1980s became the decade of ever-evolving, ever-changing government 'schemes' to try and get people off the dole. These additional counselling sessions also offered advice to workers about what to do (and what not to do) with the redundancy money. As the calendar clicked off those final few weeks leading up to the end of March we passed through all manner of these seminars designed to try and help us in some way. A few days before, on 21 March, an advice sheet had been handed to workers containing information about pensions, final wages, references and benefit entitlements. The handwritten and photocopied document was described at the time as scrappy and full of errors by the union leaders.[78]

For a good while it seemed as though every initiative offered to the soon-to-be-redundant railwaymen was viewed with a degree of cynicism. When men were questioned about their employment prospects, I remember the typical response from the more mature men being, 'Most jobs these days are in flaming offices.' This reflected the growing realisation that the changing diversity of employment in the town was going to make finding another job extremely difficult for the redundant men – even for those who qualified as being skilled. There was little comfort for the men who visited their local Job Centre to discuss their employment prospects:

> The closure of the works will have a disastrous effect on employment in the town. It's a bombshell! Even those with skills will find it hard to find alternative work. Clerical people won't have the same issues and should be absorbed without too many problems.
>
> Rodger Fowler, Swindon Job Centre manager, 1986

There was a glimmer of hope for some of the condemned men when the workshop manager at the Selhurst Depot in south London let it be known that he desperately needed vehicle body finishers and coach painters.

Twice I made the journey to Selhurst with a couple of colleagues to be interviewed and to look around the works. The idea seemed tempting, just for the opportunity to remain in work at a time of high unemployment, but with such a young family I decided that the hours spent travelling to and fro would probably damage my health, and probably my marriage! Vehicle builder Tony Rima did take the opportunity to carry on working at Selhurst and gives us an insight into the demands on his time that this arrangement involved:

> Along with half-a-dozen others I transferred to the Selhurst Depot in London; firstly on days, and then on nights. It was a ridiculous thing to do really, as on days we caught the 4:30am train and got home at 8pm. On nights, we caught the 7:30pm train and returned to Swindon at 10am! It was filthy work too; mainly fitting refurbished locks on the slam-doors.

This punishing schedule would prove to be just too much for a lot of the long-service men, who were very pessimistic about their employment prospects. Fitter Brian Phillips, whose father and brother had both been inside at the same time as him, now had two sons who were both apprentice fitters. Speaking to the *Evening Advertiser* shortly after the closure announcement, the sons asserted they could both see a future for themselves in Swindon, but for Brian it would not be so easy: 'I don't think Honda will want people over 40. I'm too old for the silicon chip. I could be at the end of the road already – at 48!'

Throughout the works, and with a measure of instinctive pride, the men continued to do their jobs until every last one was completed. Chris Rees was on hand in No. 9 Shop to photograph the final English Electric 6KT power unit being lifted out of the stand for transportation to No. 25 Shop for fitting to the last Class 8 Shunter to be overhauled at Swindon works, while Ted Jefferies took the opportunity to photograph the locomotive itself. Ted also posed in front of the final Class 03 shunting locomotive to be refurbished shortly before the closure.

And so it came to pass that 143 years of engineering excellence in Swindon Works was finally ended on 26 March 1986, the day that came to be known as Black Wednesday. Works Committee Chairman Graham Humphries told the soon-to-be-redundant workers via the local paper to

Above: No. 08675 Class 8 shunter – the final locomotive to be overhauled at Swindon Works. (E.J. Jefferies Collection)

Left: Ted Jefferies on the left with Alf Neat and John Sandford. (B.J. Nicolle Collection)

'March out with your heads held high'. They were effectively being told to walk out of the works' West Gate together in a mass exodus to mark the end of 143 years of railway engineering history in the town. 'We are asking the lads not to slink away from the works but to go out together, with pride. We don't want 150 years of history to end with a whimper.'

The reality was that when that infamous day arrived there was very little fuss, no drama and very few tears. Unlike Hugh Freebury's 'Black Fridays', whereby the men were shocked to the point of tears upon receiving their notices, the employees who went down the slope on Black Wednesday had already had far too long to get used to the fact that it was over. The local paper was issued that day with the banner headline 'Out of steam', an indication that the hard-fought battle to save the works was finally over. In truth, the employees had long been defeated by this stage, having been worn down by long months of waiting and wondering.

As it was, there was no mass march out from the West Gate that day. The BREL flag flew at half mast, while the men tended to leave in dribs and drabs, having been paid out at intervals. Committee Secretary Terry Larkham was philosophical when speaking to the local press. 'The men have their pride and feel as though they have done enough marching.' It was reported that more than £7 million walked out of the works that day after the workers had collected their final pay packets.[79]

Although a good many men were upset, Black Wednesday was more of a display of bitterness than of tears. Speaking to the *Swindon Evening Advertiser* on 26 March, Works Committee member David Rees asserted that the workforce had been betrayed by the management nationally: 'We have given the management all that we have and are now being sold down the river.' With more than 11,000 people already on the dole in Swindon at that time, he considered the outlook for the workers losing their jobs that day to be very bleak. Works Committee Secretary Terry Larkham wore a black tie, for as far as he was concerned it was a funeral and he made it known as such: 'This is a funeral; it's the death of the works. It's Black Wednesday. The lads are heartbroken and bitter because we had proved there was no reason to close us down! What is happening here today is criminal!'

Of the 1,900-plus jobs that were being lost owing to the closure announcement of 16 May 1985, only 946 actually occurred on Black Wednesday, with almost 800 of that number residing in the Swindon urban area.[80] More than 900 had either taken early retirement or found new jobs during the run-down period. Another 400–450 employees were to be retained for up to a year to keep the Spring Shop in operation and to carry out essential maintenance tasks. It has since been affirmed that the redundancy programme mainly affected older men – well over half of those made redundant being over 44 years of age. Only 55 per cent of those redundant employees possessed a recognised trade qualification.[81]

Inside the main office building that day there were others whose priorities were somewhat different. For apprentice pipefitter Ryan Conduit, his experience of Black Wednesday was memorable for more reasons than one:

> On the run down to closure I was still an apprentice. On the final day I was in the training room filling out my log book for Ken Dann the Training Officer to sign off on and effectively end my apprenticeship. I had my log books handed back just as the final hooter was sounding. I effectively had the dubious honour of being the last apprentice to come out of his time at Swindon Works.

My own experience of Black Wednesday was probably not much different to hundreds of others who exited the works for the final time that day. Having finished on my final night shift on the previous Tuesday morning, it had been decided that the whole department would report for work on that final day, at 8 a.m. No former employee who clocked on at the works for the last time on that morning could ever forget the deathly silence of that last walk through the barren workshops. I remember how the men walked slowly and sorrowfully in through the tunnel entrance that one final time, and I began to feel as though I was joining a funeral cortege midway through its mournful procession, which in a way I was. I remember walking across row upon row of empty internal rail tracks; lines that for so many years had been hives of activity and were now desolate and silent. Whichever direction I turned, my mind filled with a thousand and one memories of what had gone on before – familiar faces of smiling men, all content in their work, were now just a split-second apparition in the mind's eye. I remember looking up at those bright yellow cranes, each designed to lift 80 or 100 tons of railway carriage, and thinking their only future now was to be dismantled and sold off for scrap, along with the huge iron columns that supported the roof girders and crane tracks.

Soon to be redundant railwaymen throughout the works didn't quite know what to do with themselves. (Andy Binks, The Swindon Society)

Eventually I arrived on my section to discover all of my colleagues sat quietly in their usual places, their newspapers were unfolded as usual with their heads buried purposefully behind them, as though wishing to be alone with their private thoughts. Others, particularly the younger lads, just stood around holding onto their motorcycle helmets as though they didn't expect to be around for long, not really knowing quite what to do or what to say. Within a few hours they would be joining the swelling ranks of the unemployed outside in the real world, as they were continually being told. The chargehands I noted had purposely retired to their boxes, seemingly intent upon keeping busy, tying up any loose ends and leaving nothing unfinished. It was as though they just wanted everything to be left in perfect order, all correct and ship-shape before going down that slope for the final time. Again I thought of the *Titanic* and of 'the band that played on' with their heads held high, before the stricken vessel submerged into the murky depths.

Even on that final morning, men were occasionally being detailed to go off and finish the paintwork on some door edges or seat frames, just so that the task could be entered into the book as complete. To fill in the time, some readily complied while others just laughed and lit up another cigarette. There were a couple of senior guys out of a department of around forty or fifty men who were staying on as part of a small skeleton staff for a couple of months just to help clear the site and to see off any painting work that had remained unfinished. These men just tried to carry on as though nothing out of the ordinary was happening, purposefully keeping their thoughts to themselves as they slapped another coat of varnish onto some wooden panels. For the rest of us it was one final visit to the tea urn, those huge urns that had been boiling for as long as I can remember. We sipped our last brew silently for a while, each of us wondering how long we would be made to wait before being presented with our final redundancy payments.

As it happened, at the far end of the A Shop at least, there was none of that familiar routine of assembling the black pay tables on Black Wednesday, nor were we ever actually instructed to draw our final pay at a specific time. I remember a foreman ambling slowly across to our department sometime around mid-morning and then informing us in his most sombre voice that we could go upstairs to the office and collect our redundancy cheques and our final pay packets whenever we wanted to, and thereafter we were free to go home. I could sense among the men that there was a terrible finality about this act that made them want to put it off for as long as possible. One of the older hands commented that, 'The way he said it, it was as if he were asking a condemned man to mount the scaffold at his own convenience.' However bad anyone felt, the black humour still never ceased, right up until the end.

In some areas of the works the black pay tables were assembled one final time. Trimming Shop foreman Stan Scott was on hand to give the go-ahead for the final paying-out process to begin:

> I was a foreman on that last awful day, and the old black pay table I stood by was being filmed by a camera crew. I asked them to stand aside and give the men some quiet dignity when receiving their final pay packets. I was invited to go for a drink with the lads, but I declined and gave some excuse, but to be honest, I just felt too sickened by the whole thing.

I'd had more than enough of the sombre atmosphere by late morning, and decided I might as well go up the stairs and get my money and have done with it. My decisiveness rubbed off on a few of my colleagues and we trudged off in a group to mount the staircase together. What does it matter, I thought, I could still hang around for a while afterwards – at least until the pubs opened. When my turn finally arrived, I filed into the upstairs office and presented myself before the wages clerk, who sat behind a collection of those famous old black metal pay boxes. Within a couple of minutes, I returned back onto the department clutching a cheque for around £5,500, plus about £850 quid in £50 notes as payment of wages, plus the week-in-hand and holidays owing, etc. This was a considerable sum back in 1986, but when you had a young family to keep, a mortgage to pay and no job to go to and unemployment was running at around 3½ to 4 million, it was a mere spoonful of sugar that could only temporarily sweeten the bitterest of pills. We were also given a letter containing details of the preserved benefits in relation to our railway pension that, in my case, would in all likelihood be frozen for the next forty years. A lot of fuss had been made in the local press about Swindon being 'awash with redundancy money in the coming weeks'. The average pay-out amounted to around £7,000 (roughly £20,000 today), while the highest payments were upwards of £12,000 (£34,500 today). Works Committee Chairman Graham Humphries poured cold water on any ideas local businesses might have had of a spending spree: 'The money is not so much a golden handshake, but rather a brass one!'[82]

After chatting for a few minutes about what each of us had received, and joking about what we might and might not do with the money, we again reached that low point whereby we could no longer stand the dejecting effect of just hanging around the place for no obvious reason. A new life outside the works had to begin sometime, so why not now, at this very minute! Why put ourselves through this any longer than we have to? It was hard for us all to feel upbeat about the future while we stood there in that vast building of a thousand and one, mostly good, memories. It wasn't only the working memories that were uppermost in our minds. Most of us had worked there throughout the best years of our young lives, got married when we worked there and had become fathers for the first time when we worked there. It probably struck most of us that day, more than at any other time, how deeply the rail works had become woven into the histories of our lives almost as much as it had with some of the older hands. All over the works that day there were men in tears and I had no desire to take one final walk around the workshops to witness the degree of upset and sadness that Ryan Conduit still remembers:

> I will never ever forget the total sadness of some of those guys I saw openly crying before leaving for the last time. I have never worked in another place like the rail works where the comradeship was so close and the atmosphere so friendly.

As the clock ticked towards midday I knew then that I had to get out. I gathered up a couple of colleagues who felt the same way and we wandered off through that same tunnel entrance through which I had first entered the works around nine years earlier. I deliberately never looked back and went directly towards the Wild Deer pub on Westcott Place, where we stayed right up until closing time that afternoon. I remember we occasionally indulged in a spot of black humour in an effort to try and raise our spirits, but we mostly kept our private thoughts to ourselves and tried to present an upbeat front. For whatever reason, this infamous day did not feel like the right day for making plans for our futures, or to be talking about what we were going to do with our redundancy money. We would have plenty of time to decide about those things tomorrow and the day after.

All the pubs around the Rodbourne area were full to bursting following our final exit from the works. The TV cameras caught up with a number of electricians enjoying a final pint or two together in a local club, and one or two of them didn't hold back during their interviews:

> I'm fifty and it's going to be very, very difficult to get a job at fifty. What did Norman Tebbit say in his wisdom? We should, 'Get on our bikes to look for a job.' That's all very well, but why should we uproot our families when there is a perfectly good railway factory right there going to waste?[83]

Others among them expressed their utter disgust at the level of age discrimination that would hold some of the redundant railmen back from getting a fresh start elsewhere:

> I had 15 years of experience in contracting before I entered the rail works. When I reapplied for contracting work, they said I was too old at 38, as they only employ people aged 25–30 because they are 'quicker'. I think that's disgusting! I would back myself to keep up with anyone. It's bloody wrong that at thirty-nine you could be told that you are too old to do the job you have been doing since you left school.[84]

Back at the Wild Deer we drained away the last of our beer and shook hands across the table. Whether it was out of a sense of bitterness at the situation I cannot really say, but I said goodbye to those two workmates that day and I never ever set eyes on either of them again.

I decided to walk the mile or so distance to my house, and as I walked slowly down Wootton Bassett Road I heard the works hooter let out one long final blast that signalled the end of the line for the Swindon Railway Works. At that moment it dawned on me that from here onwards everything would be forever just a memory, nothing more.

I eventually arrived home to a house filled with the sound of children playing and my wife vacuuming as though it was just any other day. I don't remember how much beer I had drunk, but it had little or no effect as I sat staring into space for several minutes while the activity went on around me. It wasn't the worry over whether I would find another job that occupied my mind, it was the realisation that I would never again sit inside the gang hut laughing along with my workmates nor would I ever again see the inside of that mighty A Shop. Later that afternoon, the bells of St Mark's Church in Church Place, completed in 1845 to serve the workers of the Great Western Railway, rang one solitary, mournful peel, and that was that. Unfortunately I wasn't around to hear it; for me, after 143 years of railway engineering in the town, Swindon Works had already reached the end of the line. It was a very sad day.

Redundant employees heading home after the final shift on 26 March 1986. (*Swindon Advertiser*)

10

BRAVE NEW WORLD

For a number of employees, around 450 in total, life on the 'outside' would not begin for anything up to a year. Those that stayed on at the works still remember the feeling of utter desolation when the redundant men had exited the works for the final time on Black Wednesday. Stan Scott, originally a Trimming Shop foreman, found it all difficult to bear. He had stayed on in planning and estimating until March 1987 to finish off orders that were outstanding, and to deal with requests from all over the railway network to supply items that were still in demand. The worst experience for him was after the final paying-out when most of the lads had gone for the last time.

> I stood in the A Shop by the traverser table in that vast empty space and hardly a soul was around except a couple of others and John Woodman, the superintendent, overseeing the final year. Throughout the remainder of the year I experienced a terrible feeling of loss, having seen all those tradesmen now gone.

Others who were not being kept on had found the act of finally exiting the works for the final time extremely difficult. Ted Jefferies had a proud career to speak of during his thirty-plus years in Swindon Works. Firstly as an electrician, and thereafter to a position in the Training Office, Ted also became the man to take visitors around the works. Whether it was pop stars, politicians, a Poet Laureate, or groups of the general public and rail enthusiasts, they were all treated to Ted's encyclopedic knowledge of the history and workings inside. I don't think a day went by without me seeing

Ted showing visitors around, meaning he became one of the most familiar faces in the whole of the works. Ted's son, Mark, remembers how difficult it was for his father to finally leave the works on 'Black Wednesday'. His account below brings home exactly how it felt for those who had spent the majority of their working life inside Swindon Works:

> As one of the last few to finally walk out of the Rodbourne Road gates, Ted had spent the last two years of his career in Swindon Works as the curator and collator of the many historical artefacts that had accrued over the hundred-and-forty plus years that Swindon Works had existed. On his final day he went home a broken man and wept his heart out. It took a couple of years for him to recover fully and to get on with his life in retirement.

Meanwhile, in the Training Office, module controller Kevin Weaver had overseen the last of the apprentices coming out of their time during the run up to the closure, then he stayed on for a year as one of a small skeleton staff in the main office building: 'I wandered over to 19 Shop after everyone had left and it was like the *Mary Celeste*. I just felt terrible. There was not a sound. I just turned around and went home there and then. It shook me.'

Ryan Conduit had finally managed to complete his apprenticeship on that final day before the works closed, and was offered a job as a pipefitter/plumber as a part of the run-down team.

> The day after the works had closed I reported to 34 Shop, where I had been offered a position as a pipefitter/plumber as a part of the wind down team. It was eerie walking through those deserted workshops, as though you were walking through a ghost town. We spent the whole day shutting-off things that people had left on – blanking gas feeds, turning off water stopcocks, etc. In the weeks that followed we were given many other tasks including whitewashing the windows, repairing leaks and filling underground fuel tanks with concrete. I commandeered an old dumper truck and drove it around the works wearing a Davy Crockett hat. There was never a dull moment and no two days were the same.

For some of the men who remained behind to fulfil the last requirements, the feeling of bitterness continued for many months afterwards. For foreman

Stan Scott, the realisation that the closure had been utterly senseless never went away as he reflected on the decision thirty-four years later.

> I remember on one occasion getting the key to the blacksmith's shop to see if it was intact, having received a request for some items required on the network, and looking through the staff list to see if any smithys had stayed on. We closed with a potentially full order book. I've seen articles saying we did not win any orders; this is simply not true. We won many orders, but were only allowed to manufacture items until April 1987.

For those of us starting our new life on the outside, April was not really the time for allowing oneself the luxury of taking a holiday, so the search for a new position had to continue in earnest. The events of that terrible day would have to be quickly forgotten, as there were too many out of work to allow the grass to grow under one's feet. Any thoughts of self-pity would have to be at once abandoned in the desperate scramble to avoid becoming just another long-term statistic in a country of fast-approaching 4 million unemployed. Swindon's unemployment rate at that time was running at just over 14.8 per cent, which made the process of finding alternative employment extremely difficult.[85]

As bitterly as the former employees had felt the closure of the works, I remember that throughout the town in general there seemed to have been no extended period of grieving over the loss of the works. Prior to the closure, I overheard local car salesmen and electrical retailers indecently bracing themselves in anticipation of the huge sales that they could expect in a town that would be awash with redundancy money. They obviously didn't know railway workers too well, many of whom had been given sound expert advice on all manner of things when they finally went off into the outside world – including what to do with their redundancy money. Aside from that, I'd met very few people inside who could be described as frivolous when it came to spending money.

The Swindon Development Agency had been set up to look after the ongoing needs of the redundant railway workers. This included a financial package of £1.25 million, but for many of the older men – those with railway-specific skills – the likelihood that they would never work again had long since hit home. Other men of working age who went down the slope on Black Wednesday would be entering a world in which engineering jobs were scarce, and consideration would have to be given to the possibility of using their money to start up a business and going self-employed. For younger men emerging from the works, also with near obsolete skills, they might have to consider a period of retraining; either brushing up on their existing skills, or learning a completely new set.

Of course, there were those who took early retirement, and the great many who settled into an indefinite period of drawing the dole until things began to improve. I remember being staggered by the length of the alphabetically arranged dole queues when I first signed on. Was this the detritus of the Thatcher government's programme of annihilation upon the UK's nationalised industries? Even though it was below the national average, unemployment in Swindon was still considered high at around that time (7,221 unemployed following the closure of the works).[86] I remember feeling a measure of humiliation when my turn arrived to approach the desk to sign on, and there was very little empathy from Department of Health and Social Security (DHSS) staff, who themselves became more demoralised as the hand-out queues continued to lengthen. The Job Centre boards were almost completely barren of anything suitable for a skilled manual worker unless you fancied a very long commute or would consider relocation.

As for those like myself who at first shunned the retraining and start-up schemes, preferring instead to try our luck in the real world, at first a kind of 'Micawberist' approach took hold, the misguided belief that 'something will always turn up'. 'Never mind,' we would say when we bumped into each other in the town centre, 'something will eventually turn up.'[87] However, just like Wilkins Micawber in Dickens' great classic *David Copperfield*, that 'something' never did turn up, and very soon we were enrolling on those retraining schemes before the time limit to register had elapsed and left us out in the cold. I remember that I only signed on twice, before opting for a period of retraining. I trained for several months as an electrician under the auspices of the Manpower Services Commission. Most of the redundant railwaymen who continued to avoid such schemes, preferring instead to actively look for work, would have felt a bit bemused by the lack of realistic opportunities that were open to them. Even while I retrained, I still continued to search for a proper job, scanning the situations vacant pages of the *Evening Advertiser* every Thursday hoping for something that might offer a glimmer of hope. The few jobs that were available were not the kind we were looking for. I wasted many hours applying for maintenance jobs in office buildings, one of several hundred applying for a single handyman's job, usually at some large financial corporation. Unless you were prepared to take a security guard job on offer at just £2 an hour, the wait for something to turn up continued on until the next Thursday's *Evening Advertiser*. Whatever engineering companies that remained in Swindon were simply not recruiting, trying to persevere and stay afloat with whatever workforce they had. These were very dark days indeed to be looking for work, and because there were so many of us applying for a single job it became very easy to feel worthless and undervalued. I remember Peter Gabriel and Kate Bush were riding high in the pop charts with their ballad about the scourge of unemployment *Don't Give Up*. Determined *not* to give up, I finally got an interview for a buildings maintenance job with a well-known Swindon company that went very well, and I was invited to have tea with the guys who would be my new workmates. 'We will send you your contract and start date later in the week,' the boss man said. I waited and waited until a fortnight had passed – still nothing. I eventually rang the front desk only to be told quite bluntly that, 'The vacancy has been cancelled.' That is the moment that almost brings a grown man to tears, believe me!

Very soon, the realisation set in among us that Swindon had long since moved on, not only from its dependence on railway engineering, but from manufacturing employment in general. During my early days as a social science undergraduate in the mid-1990s, I remember one particular lecturer identifying Swindon as 'the prime example of a town that had experienced severe social, cultural, political and economic effects on the path from slump to boom'. Any former employee of the town's railway workshops still out there searching for a job would know exactly what he meant, for at that time the uniqueness of Swindon referred, not solely to its 'railway culture,' but to that aforementioned successful transition from a town bearing all the characteristics of a northern industrial town to a thriving economic centre of commerce and multinational expansion. Even by the time the railway works had closed down its operations, the town of Swindon had been a town in transition for some fifteen years, with economic and social change very much in evidence. Much had already been done behind the scenes in council chambers when the collapse of manufacturing employment in the early 1970s had already begun to bite. The subsequent rise in unemployment led to a sharp policy reassessment, leading to a new industrial promotion strategy; 'Swindon Enterprise' was set up as a semi-autonomous marketing agency to promote the town. The emphasis had been on attracting hi-tech companies, office headquarters and other profitable concerns that did not need development area subsidies to survive. The development of campus-style business parks was explicitly encouraged throughout the development process.[88]

As if things didn't already look bleak enough for us redundant railwaymen, It was clear that throughout the 1980s there had been a major downturn in the economy nationally, and it was manufacturing employment that generally bore the brunt. This was particularly evident in Swindon, where this form of employment continued to decline rapidly, while at the same time service employment increased significantly as the town continued along that path of very successful diversification. Because of this, it appears as though Swindon came through the loss of the works relatively unscathed with statistics bolstered by those huge increases in service employment. As the technological bubble continued to expand there was also strong growth in electrical and electronic engineering employment locally, while insurance, finance and business employment rose by 29 per cent, compared with 17 per cent nationally, with the creation of some 2,800 jobs.[89] I remember earning a few extra pounds myself at these electronic companies, mainly doing soul-destroying weekend night shifts packing microchips into clear plastic tubes ready for distribution.

As the 1980s wore on this alarming growth continued in financial services as the biggest player, Allied Dunbar expanded its Swindon facility significantly. There was also a glimmer of hope for those looking for a new start in engineering when Japanese giant Honda set up a pre-sales service facility, as well as an engine manufacturing facility, on the site of the old Vickers airfield. There was much speculation at the time that a major car assembly plant would follow, which it eventually did. There is a certain irony that, as I write this some thirty-three years later, an announcement had just been made that the Honda facility is to close with the loss of 3,500 jobs!

On the face of it, it appears that while the Swindon Works decayed and died, the rest of the town was continuing the transformation that had begun before I first entered the railway works. Much of this can be put down to the aforementioned strategic location of the town making it ideally placed to benefit from government worries over rapid population growth in the south-east, and the resulting pressure for development beyond London's green belt. The enthusiastic response of the local council in Swindon, coupled with an impressive track record of successful expansion, had previously led to the town being singled out after a series of high-level planning studies as early as the mid-1960s. Few realised that Swindon had already been designated as the site of a proposed expansion from a population of around 100,000 to 250,000 by 1981, and was set to further increase to 400,000 by 2001. This was later revised down to 150,000 by 1986 owing to the harsh economic recession of the mid-1970s. Current estimates are now 265,400 by 2031.[90]

Swindon also became a major beneficiary of the ever-increasing internationalisation of the UK economy. It is interesting how existing companies in Swindon facilitated their own survival by capitalising not only on the strategic importance of the town but particularly on this wider internationalisation of the free market. The Austin-Rover plant at Pressed Steel successfully exploited production opportunities in league with both Saab and Volvo and, ultimately, with Honda, thus decreasing the plant's dependence upon the parent company for keeping it afloat. Plessey also refocused its activities towards the lucrative semiconductor market, employing more than 750 workers in 1987 in its drive towards operating successfully within what was a highly competitive field. Inward investment by foreign-owned companies increased rapidly into the 1980s, particularly from the US multinationals who, by the mid-1980s, had increased their share of manufacturing employment in the town to 27 per cent.[91] It is often claimed that Swindon Works was selected for closure because it was felt that the town could recover a lot easier from the massive job losses than other railway towns. I very much dispute this view, simply because a couple of years earlier BREL had no compunction about closing Shildon Works in County Durham which was more of a one-industry town than Swindon – particularly with the coal mining being very much in decline.

Despite the widespread 'knuckle down and accept it' approach to the situation among the people of Swindon, there was never any suggestion that the Swindon Works should just simply be forgotten as the town moved on. Everybody knew that the Great Western Railway and Swindon Works would forever endure as the heritage of the Swindon community. For a century and a half the railway culture had touched the lives of virtually all who lived in Swindon to varying degrees, in much the same way as mining had done in South Wales and Yorkshire and in other communities. This identification with the railway workshops was never going to end with the events of Black Wednesday. Despite the fact that the mighty A Shop, because of its enormous size, had already been earmarked for demolition, much of the original character of the remaining buildings that comprised the railway works would be preserved almost intact up to the present day. Eleven of the original units were designated as Grade II listed buildings shortly before the closure of the works. These eleven buildings, along with five other original GWR buildings, formed a significant collection of sixteen structures that effectively showcased the historical development of the works from the 1840s onwards.[92]

In 1987 the railway village and engineering works was formally designated as a conservation area 'of special architectural or historic interest the character of which it is desirable to preserve or enhance'. Thereafter, the Swindon Borough Council was required to pay special attention to the need to preserve or enhance the character and appearance when considering whether to grant planning permission for development within the said conservation area. In line with the 1990 Act, it was also required to draw up and publish proposals for the preservation and enhancement of the area.

The works and railway village's status as an area of significant historical importance rests upon two important criteria. Firstly, the area now exists as one of Britain's finest monuments to the early days of the railway age, and part of one of the most significant surviving historic railway establishments in the world. This includes the area's historical relationship with the adjacent 'railway village' – a purpose-built area of terraced housing and essential facilities built exclusively for the GWR workforce. Situated to the south of the former works, the development eventually came to be designated as the Swindon Railway Village Conservation Area.

Second, there is also considerable historic interest in the architectural form of the area's surviving industrial and administrative buildings, many of which display innovatory forms of construction and exemplify the style of industrial building typical of its period (*c.*1840–1920). The form, size and construction of the buildings typically reflected the activities to be performed within. The fact that they are generally very large and single-storey contrasts sharply with the multi-storey mills and warehouses commonly associated with the early days of the industrial revolution. The aforementioned railway village also survives virtually intact, providing a rare example of early Victorian planning and

A boiler belonging to No. 34072 Class BB *257 Squadron* sits rusting on the gravel, while the mighty A Shop is slowly being demolished in the background. (Brian Robert Marshall)

architectural style. The 300 limestone cottages, originally designed by Brunel and built between 1840 and 1880, had looked doomed to demolition as most of them had fallen into disrepair. Swindon Council eventually bought the village from British Rail before undertaking an award-winning refurbishment. The entire conservation area in question covers more than 21 hectares at the heart of the land once covered by the former GWR works.

By the end of June 1987, the remainder on the BREL workforce had finally left the site, and after a considerable period when nothing seemed to be happening, it was announced that a £9 million bid had been accepted from a consortium including White Horse Holdings to take over the premises. The original plan was for the Swindon Development Agency and Swindon Enterprise Trust to facilitate the setting up of starter industries in an effort to get people back into work. Then at the eleventh hour it was announced that White Horse Holdings had pulled out of the deal and the contract to take over the site was then awarded to the Midlands development company Tarmac Properties in 1987. In total, Tarmac had purchased 142 acres of former railway works land, and plans for the development of a shopping mall were already in place by December of that year. The project had to be sidelined a year later owing to the collapse of the commercial property market, and then finally in January 1994 approval was granted for the construction of the 200,000 sq ft McArthurGlen Designer Outlet Village that has now been masterfully inserted into the vast 1870s engineering building without damage to, or removal of any of its original features. Regrettably, a lot of the machinery from the railway works had already been shipped off to India and Bangladesh, although there are still a few intriguing examples of old railway machinery exhibited throughout the centre as though they were modern works of art. The project has been described by heritage experts as possibly the single most ambitious conversion of a former railway building in the whole of the UK. The general offices, also listed Grade II, now form the National Monuments Record Centre (NMRC) and offices for English Heritage. The former Locomotive Works Manager's office, now known as Churchward House, was refurbished for continued office use.

Grandson indicating his grandad! The 'wall of names' was erected inside STEAM: Museum of the Great Western Railway as a tribute to the thousands of rail workers who passed through the Swindon Works. Thereafter, descendants proudly identify the names of their ancestors.

In the same month that we celebrate the sixtieth anniversary of the final steam locomotive *Evening Star*, we also count off thirty-four years that have now passed since Black Wednesday back in 1986. The entire railway works area has for many years been going through its own long period of transition, a process that required transforming the near-derelict industrial site that we vacated in 1986 to the mixed use public urban realm that was then envisioned for the future. The change in the use of the site and its buildings has, of course, affected its traditional character and appearance, but change need not be considered contrary to good conservation practice. To date, all of the apparent changes so far undertaken appear to have preserved or enhanced the identity of the former works as a historic industrial site of national importance. The most significant move towards the permanent commemoration of the works

Early morning shoppers enjoy coffee alongside a Swindon-built Manor-class locomotive on the site that was once Swindon Works. (Ron Bateman)

came about when the former Nos 19 and 20 shops were converted for the setting up of STEAM: Museum of the Great Western Railway, which opened its doors in June 2000. Costing around £11 million, the 70,000 sq ft museum was opened by HRH Prince Charles, who had taken a particular interest in the initiatives to preserve the old railway buildings. He conceded that over the years he had watched in despair as Britain's industrial heritage had been mercilessly swept away to make room for redevelopment.

Protracted discussions on how to utilise the remaining buildings continue to this day. Because the area west of Rodbourne Road contained buildings mainly from the early twentieth century expansion of the works, and the area east of the Gloucester railway line contained little of historic interest, it was felt that conservation-area status for these two areas, west and east of the core, could not be justified.

Now that it is all gone, and the old railway buildings have been converted to alternative use, it is difficult to gauge what measure of pride that each new generation of Swindonians attach to their railway heritage. The artefacts on display at the outlet village, coupled with the STEAM Museum with its impressive 'wall of names', make it unlikely that the works and the men who served inside will ever be forgotten. Social media has also helped to keep the memory of the works, and in particular the Training School, alive. Andy Hodson's comment sums up how many feel when they look back at their time in the works: 'It was a seriously sad day when it closed. You don't realise how good you had it until it's gone. The best job I ever had!'

Chris Smithson wondered how many of us would still be there today had it still been open; 'Would we have ever left if it hadn't closed? Never in a million years. Never had another job like it!'

Regrettably there is one unwanted legacy of the works that will live on in the minds of many bereaved families of the former railway employees. Mesothelioma is a particularly aggressive form of cancer linked to asbestosis, and has taken the lives of many of the town's former railwaymen. Because it is considered a much rarer disease in other parts of the country, it eventually came to be dubbed 'the Swindon Disease' with the cause rooted firmly within the town's former railway works. Asbestos was used extensively in the workshops. Its valuable properties (lack of conductivity and an inability to burn) made it the perfect heat insulator. Vast quantities of the material were present as it was the main source of heat insulation used, often sandwiched between two strips of metal in the boiler casing, and utilised as lagging around the pipe work. The carriages contained asbestos and even the actual workshops themselves had asbestos lagging on every pipe as they were heated by steam. In the 1960s, when the railway industry entered the diesel era, the trains were sprayed with asbestos and a thick fog of the substance often hung over every engine workshop. Exposure came mainly from inhaling or unintentionally ingesting the dust. Tony Rima took the opportunity to record his experience of being exposed to asbestos in the early 1960s when he was transferred into the body shop where he learned to weld:

> It was here that I was exposed unknowingly to blue asbestos. A new type of coach had just been introduced that was made of steel, and we had to cut away any rusted sections of panel work and weld on new sections. We were not told that the insulation used was asbestos and that it was deadly, even though British Rail had stopped using it some years before. It is something I feel very angry about, as we were not given any protective

Swindon STEAM: Museum of the Great Western Railway – now home to the pride of Swindon Works, *King George V.* (Ron Bateman)

Works Training School reunion; September 2012. The 1977 intake L-R: Alan Redford, Nigel Sheriden, Robert Authbert, Colin Everall, Ron Bateman.

clothing or masks to wear – only the totally ineffective Martindale mask was available, which was for nuisance dust only.

Tony Rima

Tragically, Tony was diagnosed with mesothelioma in 2008 and died in 2010. During discussions about his incredible photographic legacy, his daughter Samantha made the very poignant remark, 'My dad loved the railways, and it was the very thing that killed him.' The additional fact that it is an illness caused by hard work makes it seem particularly unfair. Some workers would be required to scrape the substance from the inside of boilers and then go home covered in toxic dust – completely unaware of its potential side effects. The substance was also reusable, meaning employees would pull it off, soak it in water then put it in a kind of cement mixer to prepare the asbestos to be reapplied to the boiler and all the pipe work. I have been told by more than one former rail worker that they would often playfully flick it at one another – totally unaware of the hazardous nature of the substance. The men working with the blue asbestos were in the most danger because the material was much finer. Prior to the late 1950s, workers were given no protective equipment – not even the most basic masks referred to by Tony Rima above. Throughout the years following the closure of the workshops, the countless compensation claims against British Rail became a regular feature in the local press. The high incidence of the disease has meant that the numbers of former GWR railwaymen about the town who can provide such wonderful recollections of 'God's Wonderful Railway' began disappearing at an alarming rate. Mesothelioma was being diagnosed in 2,000 people nationwide every year.[93] Often described as a time bomb, the disease usually occurs forty years after a person has stopped working with the hazardous material. Because of the debilitating nature of the disease it is always very distressing for the family to watch a loved one going slowly downhill. It is very much a silent killer, and thankfully the number of cases in the UK was forecast to reduce significantly after 2015.

In April 2003, a memorial garden was set up in Queens Park in Swindon's Old Town to commemorate thousands of people who have lost their lives to mesothelioma.

ENDNOTES

INTRODUCTION

1. Roberts, H., 'How works tore up the rules and prospered', *Swindon Evening Advertiser*, 22 May 1985.
2. Bassett, K., Boddy, M., Harloe, M., Lovering, J., (1994 ed.) 'Economic and Social Changes in Swindon', in Anderson, J., Ricci, M. (1994 ed.) *Society and Social Science – A Reader*, The Open University, Milton Keynes, p.215.
3. *Swindon Evening Advertiser* supplement, 1 April 2006.
4. Reily, R.C. (1996) *The Heyday of Swindon and its Locomotives*, Ian Allan, Shepperton, p.4.
5. Freebury, H. (1985) *Great Western Apprentice: Swindon in the Thirties*, Wiltshire County Council publications, Trowbridge. pp.143–144.
6. 'Lessons of History: An illusion of Railway Grandeur', *The Independent*, 22 March 1993.
7. Gourvish, T.R. (2018) *British Railways 1948–73: A Business History*, Cambridge University Press.
8. A Guinea was equal to 21 shillings (£1.05 today). The winners would each have received £3 10*s*.
9. Letter to *Railway Magazine*, August 2016.
10. Fuller, F. (1987) *The Railway Works and Church in New Swindon*, Red Brick, Swindon, p.49.
11. Figures for 1965/69 quoted in Matheson, R. (2016) *Swindon Works: The Legend*, The History Press, Stroud. Figure for 1963 quoted in Roberts, H. (1985) 'How works tore up the rules and prospered', *Evening Advertiser*, 22 May 1985.
12. Gourvish (2018).

13. In late 2009 a new mystery sprang up around the locomotive when it was suggested that following a mishap with a tank engine, it was withdrawn from service and swapped identities and boilers with a classmate. Fuel was added to the rumours when work was carried out on a sister locomotive, 92203 *Black Prince*, which revealed that beneath the black paint was some of *Evening Star's* Brunswick Green paint and that some parts were stamped 92220.
14. Binks, A., Timms, P. (2015), *Swindon Works Through Time*, Amberley, Stroud.
15. Although Maybach engines were fitted to many Warships and Western-class locomotives, Andy Woodward has asserted that at least two Mercedes-Benz engines were used in a Western Class 52 hydraulic and one in a Warship Class 42.
16. BREL was finally privatised in 1989.
17. *RailTalk*, special edition, April/May 1982.
18. Freebury, H. (1985).
19. Exchange of letters between H. Freebury and K.J. Cook OBE, Mechanical and Electrical Engineer of Swindon Works and author of *Swindon Steam – 1921–1951* in Freebury (1985), pp.159–163.

CHAPTER 1

20. Bassett, K., Boddy, M., Harloe, M., Lovering, J. (1994 ed) 'Economic and Social Changes in Swindon', in Anderson, J., Ricci, M. (1994 ed) *Society and Social Science: A Reader,* The Open University, Milton Keynes. p.216.
21. Ibid., pp.216–217.
22. Ibid., p.221.
23. *Swindon Evening Advertiser*, 3 December 1977.
24. Works Manager Harry Roberts decided that the children's TV programme *Blue Peter* should have the rights to exclusively report on the discovery in a programme aired in May 1975. After going on show at the Swindon Museum, where it attracted more than 5,000 visitors, the specimen was ultimately donated to the British Museum following the 1975 Swindon Works Open Days.
25. Roberts (1985).
26. *Swindon Evening Advertiser*, 9 March 1977.
27. Ibid.
28. *Swindon Advertiser,* 5 June 2008.
29. Kitchen Sink Drama: A cultural movement that developed in theatre and cinema in Britain during the late 1950s and extended into television during the early 1960s. Productions typically reflected the domestic situations of working-

class Britons residing in cramped, run-down inner suburbs. The style has since been described as social realism.

30. The first pocket-sized electronic calculator was the Busicom LE-120A Handy, which became available in 1971. Manufactured in Japan, it was also the first calculator to use an LED display.

31. Pig roast, Beatrice Street (1977). *Swindon Advertiser*, 10 July 2008.

32. Harold J. Fleming attended Warminster Theological College between leaving the railway works and turning profession with Swindon Town FC. *This is Wiltshire* @web.archive.org

33. Geoffrey Boycott, former Yorkshire and England cricketer, scored 8,114 Test match runs for England in 108 Tests between 1964 and 1982. He had just scored his 100th hundred on 11 August 1977.

34. Long after the Swindon Works had closed, I acted in the capacity of a workers' representative at another engineering firm for almost twenty years!

CHAPTER 2

35. The £1.2 billion modernisation plan that spawned the training schools also included major track and signalling improvements, and replacement of outdated steam engines with diesel and electric traction.

36. A more comprehensive account of the commissioning of the school and the new approach can be found in Matheson, R., (2011). *Doing Time Inside. Apprenticeship and Training in GWR's Swindon Works*, History Press, Stroud. pp.121–124.

37. I wished that I was getting £26.55 p/w. As an EITB-sponsored apprentice, I was only receiving £19 p/w in the form of a pink cheque.

38. (Captain) Harry Roberts recounted his wartime experiences in his book *Capture at Arnhem* (1999), Windrush Press (published posthumously).

CHAPTER 3

39. The Boeing Everett Factory covers an area of 98.3 acres (4.1 million sq ft), making it the largest building in the world by volume.

40. Those women, of course, did valuable war work; and the 'tunnel story' was probably a tall story carried on through generations of railwaymen. A number of women were kept on after the war into the 1950s to make up for the lack of available manpower. (Matheson, 2016).

41. *Metropolis*, 1927, a German science fiction film directed by Fritz Lang.

42. Red oxide paint, a specially formulated primer for ferrous metals.

CHAPTER 4

43. The module controller generally monitored the apprentices' progress and ensured that all the required specifications and phase tests were completed within the stated training period.
44. B Shed 4 – In the early days of the works, the shop numbers were designated by a letter rather than a number. No. 19 shop was originally B Shed – otherwise the Erecting and Tender Shop.
45. Wood. D., Sewell. N. (2008) *Haunted Swindon*, Beedon Books, Derby.

CHAPTER 5

46. Bryson, B. (2015) *The Road to Little Dribbling*, Penguin. London.
47. *Swindon Advertiser* supplement, 1 April 2006.

CHAPTER 6

48. *Swindon Evening Advertiser*, 1 February 1979.
49. Roberts, H., 'How works tore up the rules and prospered', *Swindon Evening Advertiser*, 22 May 1985.
50. *railmagazine.com*, 29 July 2009.
51. *Swindon Evening Advertiser*, 14 April 1982.
52. *Railnews*, 1 September 2008.
53. In the summer of 1984 BR won approval for east coast electrification all the way to Edinburgh, and the first of many new approvals for new locomotives and rolling stock, *Railnews*, 1 September 2008.

CHAPTER 7

54. Roberts, H. (1985) 'How works tore up the rules and prospered'.
55. *Daily Mirror*, 14 May 1982.
56. *Swindon Evening Advertiser*, 23 April 1982.
57. Throughout April 1982, the number employed at Swindon Works was generally reported in the local press to be in the region of 3,500.
58. *Swindon Evening Advertiser*, 7 May 1982.
59. Ibid.
60. Serpell, D. (1983) *Review of Railway Finances*, London, HM Stationery Office. pp.9–11.
61. Ibid. p.125.

62. Ibid. pp.37–40.
63. *Swindon Evening Advertiser*, 6 January 1983.
64. *Northern Echo*, 7 May 1984.
65. *Look North*, 3 August 1983.
66. *Swindon Evening Advertiser*, 2 May 1984.
67. Ibid.
68. *Swindon Advertiser*, twentieth anniversary supplement, 1 April 2006.
69. *Swindon Evening Advertiser*, 4 August 1984.
70. *Swindon Evening Advertiser*, 10 August 84.

CHAPTER 8

71. As things turned out, the works closed after just sixteen months following Works Manager Harold Taylor's promise of eighteen months' work.
72. *Swindon Evening Advertiser*, 16 May 1985.
73. Ibid.
74. Hansard, United Kingdom, *Railway Workshops Job Losses*, api.parliament.uk, House of Commons, 16 May 1985, vol. 71, p.491, David Mitchell MP, Parliamentary Under-Secretary of State for Transport.

CHAPTER 9

75. *Swindon Evening Advertiser*, 19 July 1984.
76. Princess Elizabeth toured the works on 15 November 1950. Presentation of model quoted in Matheson (2016) *Swindon Works: The Legend*, p.66.
77. Mr Coombs did in fact hold on to his seat at the next general election, and remained as Swindon's MP until 1997.
78. *Swindon Evening Advertiser*, 21 March 1986.
79. *Swindon Evening Advertiser*, 27 March 1986.
80. *The Effect of Railworks Redundancies upon Communities in Swindon*, Swindon Community Development Office, 1986.
81. Ibid.
82. *Swindon Evening Advertiser*, 25 March 1986.
83. Norman Tebbit was Secretary of State for employment in 1981–83 and Secretary of State for Trade and Industry in 1983–1985.
84. *Off the Rails*, Swindon Works BBC West, 1985.

CHAPTER 10

85. *Swindon Evening Advertiser* twentieth anniversary supplement, 1 April 2006.
86. '30 Years of Great Western Enterprise', Businesswest.co.uk. p.4.
87. Mr Micawber was a character in Charles Dickens' *David Copperfield*, who struggled through life in the belief that 'something would always turn up' to relieve him of his financial difficulties.
88. The Swindon Enterprise Trust eventually merged with the Swindon Development Agency in 1989 to form the business advisory body Great Western Enterprise.
89. Bassett, K., Boddy, M., Harloe, M., Lovering, J. (1994 ed) *Economic and Social Changes in Swindon*, in Anderson, J., Ricci, M. (1994 ed) *Society and Social Science: A Reader,* The Open University, Milton Keynes.
90. *Swindon Borough Council Population Projections to 2031,* Swindon Joint Strategic Needs Assessment, 29 May 2014.
91. Bassett, K. et al. (1994).
92. *Swindon Railway Works Conservation Area Appraisal*, Swindon Borough Council, May 23, 2006. P.10/11
93. *Swindon Advertiser*, 27 February 2006.

ACKNOWLEDGEMENTS

THE PHOTOGRAPHERS

Tony Rima

Photography had been one of Tony's main passions. As a vehicle builder in No.19A Shop, Tony had taken hundreds of photos of the works with the intention of one day publishing a book about his time inside. He was a member of the Swindon Camera Club for many years and won the coveted annual exhibition among other awards. Tony's love of photography is shared by his daughter **Samantha Baker**, who I am indebted to for allowing me access to and use of his work.

Ted Jefferies

Since his marriage in 1947 until he was too old to hold a camera, Ted was a photographer, leaving a huge archive of family and local events. There is also a large collection of photos from inside, many of which were I suspect not strictly allowed. However, most of his photography was done on film and he never could get the hang of how digital cameras could store hundreds of pictures on a little square of plastic and be reproduced on his TV screen. (Mark Jefferies)

Roy Hazell Roy was a very familiar figure around the Works Training School, having been manager of the school throughout much of its operational life. Roy compiled a series of excellent images recording 'a day in the life' of the training school. I am very grateful to **Matt Chambers** and to other members of Roy's family for granting me permission to reproduce images from his collection.

A big thank you to **Andy Binks** at the Swindon Society for sourcing images, including some of his own, that I was able to use. Also thanks to **Barrie Hudson** at the *Swindon Advertiser* for helping me to source important images from the newspaper's archive.

Other photographers I would like to thank include **Pete Gradidge**, **Keith Miller, Paul Gulliver** and **Brian Robert Marshall**. I would also like to thank **Jason McCormick** and **Neil Lover** for allowing me access to their wonderful collection on their site, Swindon's Other Railway.

I would also like to thank **John Baker** and **Colin Finch** at the Swindon Apprentice social media site for their assistance towards obtaining the best quality images, and to all the former apprentices for their valuable contributions.

Lastly, my special thanks to **Rosa Matheson** for doing me the honour of writing an excellent foreword for this publication.

Every effort has been made to trace the copyright holders. In the event of any omission, the author requests to be contacted via the publishers so it may be rectified for future editions.

INDEX